Texas Tide

Texas Tide

A Blue Print of the Future and how to survive the Tide, flowing North of the Rio Grande River.

Tony Aguilar

iUniverse, Inc.
Bloomington

Texas Tide
A Blue Print of the Future and how to survive the Tide,
flowing North of the Rio Grande River.

Copyright © 2006, 2011 Tony Aguilar

iUniverse books may be ordered through booksellers or by contacting:

iUniverse
1663 Liberty Drive
Bloomington, IN 47403
www.iuniverse.com
1-800-Authors (1-800-288-4677)

ISBN: 978-0-595-38258-3 (pbk)
ISBN: 978-0-595-84690-0 (cloth)
ISBN: 978-0-595-82628-5 (ebk)

Library of Congress Control Number: 2010902903

Printed in the United States of America

iUniverse rev. date: 2/9/2011

I'm very proud of this new book, which is unique and very revealing. The subtitle explains it best, the true blueprint is one that is reviewed and followed. Without direction, preparing for the Tide is difficult.

Texas Tide deals with allot of issues, one being the rise in the Hispanic population here in the southwest and the impact on local and state politics.

A professional once told me that writing a book simply about politics, would be a waste of time, but I disagree. First, I'm going to tell it, like I see it. And if you disagree with my views, send me your book and I'll critique it.

Lastly, I was very moved at all the support and letters that I've received concerning the health of my mother, as much as I would like, it is virtually impossible to respond to all of my well-wishers and supporters throughout the country.

It is my hope that this book will shed some insight on the Hispanic Community and act as a tool to help build bridges of friendship and outreach.

My mother always stated that food is one instrument that will always bridge cultures. So I encourage you to read and practice some of the recipes my family has utilized to bring the community together.

Tony

CREDITS
Written by:

Anthony Arthur Aguilar

Hermelinda Aguilar-Delgadillo
Anna Bertha Aguilar
Katherine Yvonne Aguilar

A special thanks to:

Dr. Frank Hendrickson
For his encouragement to me
In writing this book,

And

Ralph G. Hendrickson
For advice, editorial comments and graphics.

Contents

A Dream within a Dream

Take this kiss upon the brow!
And, in parting from you now,
Thus much let me avow—

You are not wrong, who deem
That my days have been a dream;

Yet if Hope has flown away
In a night, or in a day,
In a vision, or in none,
Is it therefore the less gone?

All that we see or seem
Is but a dream within a dream.
I stand amid the roar
Of a surf-tormented shore,

And I hold within my hand
Grains of the golden sand—
How few! Yet how they creep
Through my fingers to the deep,
While I weep—while I weep!

O God! Can I not grasp
Them with a tighter clasp?
O God! Can I not save

One from the pitiless wave?

Is all that we see or seem
But a dream within a dream?

By Edgar Allan Poe

Develop a Good Memory.

"*Sometimes life is so challenging, so painful, that it is plain impossible to feel grateful for anything that is going on. At such moments, it is nice to have a reservoir of contentment to fall back on, a storehouse of joyful memories to open and hold onto as you navigate through the dark night of the soul.*

A good memory does not just work for tough times. It also helps to smooth over the little bumps and glitches of ordinary life, particularly in relationships. When I find myself annoyed with something my husband is saying, for instance, if I can remember the piece of angel food cake he brought me as a surprise yesterday while I was working, my annoyance melts as my gratitude is engaged.

A good memory also helps, for example, when you find yourself angry with a co-worker for failing to meet a deadline. Recalling with gratitude how often she has come through for you in the past graciously let her off the hook. A good memory keeps us from losing our perspective, from being so caught up in the work of the here and now that we forget the larger bounty of our lives. I'm not suggesting that we should deny our suffering or ignore the problems in our lives, just that we can balance them with joy and peacefulness by remembering moments, events, and people that we are grateful for.

What are the things in your life that, looking back, you are most thankful for? Notice what comes up without your reaching for it. This practice is not about making a laundry list but of allowing yourself to notice what really sticks with you. These are your highlights of Happiness: the birth of your son, recovery from a serious illness, a certain way the light falls in you bedroom whatever they are, they are your precious moments to be taken out and savored any time you need them."

Attitudes of Gratitude by M.J. Ryan pg. 125

Part I
THE PAST

1

RISING TIDE

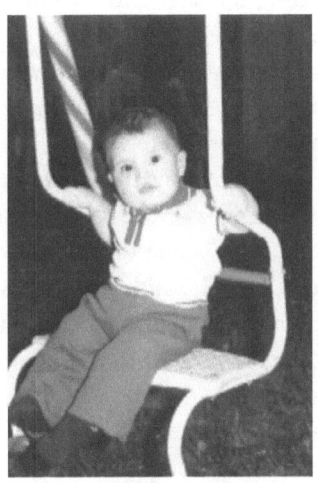

The poet called Miss Liberty's torch, "the lamp beside the golden door." Well, that was the entrance to America, and it still is. And now you really know why we are here tonight. The glistening hope of that lamp is still ours. Every promise every opportunity is still golden in this land. And through that golden door, our children can walk into tomorrow with the knowledge that no one can be denied the promise that is America. Her heart is full; her torch is still golden, her future bright. She has arms big enough to comfort and strong enough to support, for the strength in her arms is the strength of her people. She will carry on in the eighties unafraid, unashamed, and unsurpassed. In this springtime of hope, some lights seem eternal; America's is.

Ronald Reagan—RNC speech, August 23, 1984

The President said it best in the poem titled Miss Liberty's torch, opportunity and promise is here for those that have the guts to come and get it. Imagine a world where twelve million or so individuals grow in one specific area and are only held back by the oceans.

Yesterday my sister, who lives in Mexico near the Pacific Ocean, called me to tell me about her day. She talked about visiting an old aunt that lives in the countryside outside of Mexico City. Just shortly after Anna's return, to the states, Aunt Lupe rest her soul, passed away at the glorious age of 100. Anna reminded me of the time Aunt Lupe would entertain us with stories and simple little quotes, and her tales of getting up early and watching the sunrise, and working on the farm to ensure the chores were done.

Her famous quote was *"The Ocean is full of dreams, but until you get your feet wet, you'll never know what promise life has for you, so don't sit there all day,"* which we all realized was move faster or get more work.

Anna said, "You know Tony, it seems like yesterday that we were running in the fields as children. Sometimes I wish we could stop time and run for days in that field". I interrupted and said "Anna don't you remember all the bugs and heat that came with the running". She said "Shut up Ant, this is my story, let me continue. Let's see we were in the field and mother had just got us to set up the picnic blanket and thermos cooler, for us to eat. Mom always thought that having a picnic would keep us together."

Opportunity and Promise is what kept us together.

I'm sure my mother granted us the opportunity, and Aunt Lupe ensured the promise with her famous quotes. But the real questions Anna and I discussed were about the Rising Tide and influences that family and tradition play in modern day politics. So the question is how do we begin to understand the rising tide?

We can understand the tide by uniting and bridging any differences that we may have.

Many people today don't realize that Hispanics, for example, represent a good size in the total U.S. population. According to my research and study of Census data; it is shown that nearly sixty-eight percent of all Hispanics in the United States are Mexican Americans. Just imagine what the numbers are in Texas and even in the city of Dallas.

For example here in the Dallas Public Schools, I can personally say that the district is over seventy-five percent or more Hispanic. Just the other day a friend of mine commented on the growing numbers here in Dallas County.

She stated that another growing and political group are the Cuban Americans which account for about seven to eight percent with other Hispanics from Central America, South America, and Spain together make up about twenty-four percent of the Hispanic population.

Our family and others have made efforts to reach out in this new century and help clear up misunderstandings that exist in the Hispanic Community. Since the mid 90's, various groups here in Texas have reached out and made inroads with strong conservative Hispanic organizations. Sometimes the bonds shared in the family and faith in God play key roles. Mexican-Americans, Cuban-Americans, and other groups share cultural similarities that date back years.

In North Texas and probably other parts of the state, common bonds tend to be the Spanish language and the Roman Catholic Church, which are the oldest and most important cultural keys that unite Hispanics here in the Southwest.

I will admit that in the Dallas Area a growing number of non-Catholic Christian organizations have made inroads into the community.

The Southern Baptist Convention, for example, has realized the need to recruit and train ministers to promote the faith in various communities, which cater to a broad audience. Dr. Frank Hendrickson, a missionary who travels around the world, has seen a growing trend and has encouraged me to reach out to all in my community outreach. I'm honored to have been advised during my political runs for public office by so many outstanding members of the community.

Just as generations of Irish or Italians immigrants came to this country and maintained their culture, it is not unusual for Hispanic immigrants to maintain theirs. Consequently, nearly all Hispanic Americans can speak Spanish, and large majorities are Roman Catholics. Hispanics in the United States today speak a variety of Spanish dialects, depending on their country or region of origin. Nevertheless, the speakers of one dialect can usually understand the speakers of another with no difficulty.

Although some Hispanic Americans do not use Spanish at all, most continue to speak Spanish in their homes and teach the language to their children. Many adult immigrants have difficulty learning English, but their children usually grow up speaking both Spanish and English.

For example, if you go to Sulfur Springs and speak to some of the Hispanics in the community, a lot of their dialect has been modified to fit the surroundings. Chopping or splicing English words to fit into Spanish, for example rat is rata, truck is trocke.

Hispanics who are not fluent in English face obstacles in schooling and employment. Moreover, some people do not see the Hispanics as one group, a group whose ancestry and social background are different from their own. Such perceptions have led to miscommunication and false ideas regarding the community. In the community, there are people of different national and ethnic origins. Physical appearances vary widely and often show the blending of European, American Indian and African features that occurred over many generations.

Mexican Americans, for example, are mestizos, that is, they are of mixed Spanish and American Indian ancestry. Cuban-Americans are of Spanish descent, though some blacks and mulattoes also emigrated from Cuba. Over half of Hispanics live in urban areas, particularly in Los Angeles, New York City, Miami, Dallas, San Antonio, and many cities in the Southwest. Houston is also home to large groups of Hispanics from Colombia, Cuba, the Dominican Republic, and Ecuador. Mexicans form the largest Hispanic group in the Southwest.

Cities such as Houston and El Paso, Austin also has small Cuban, Guatemalan, and Puerto Rican communities. Miami, the city that never sleeps, has the largest Cuban-American population of any U.S. city.

Small towns such as Boise, Idaho, and Tulsa, Oklahoma have seen their populations increase due to Hispanic immigrants. One excellent example is in Commerce, Texas, near my alma mater Texas A&M University-Commerce. If you go down the back roads near the University you will see how small farms and older homes have been bought up and fixed by recent immigrant arrivals. It wasn't uncommon for friends of mine or myself to be working the school farm and come across some new visitors looking for work.

Sometimes a new friend would play the guitar and tell of tales of working cattle in Nebraska or riding herd in the feedlots of Amarillo.

Questions would come up about their origin and what state they were from and if they had some insight to share on making our work easier. Eventually Dr. David Crenshaw would come out and remind us that if we needed history class, we're in the wrong department. If we wanted to learn about Beef Cattle management, we needed to finish our work. Ha! I believe that semester I learned more and didn't even pass the class, now that I think about it. Now let's return to history and I'll leave my school stories for another day. Well maybe not.

One day while walking through the hallway in the Ag/Science building, I noticed my old friend Dr. David Crenshaw talking to some students about his adventures working in the Valley. He stated that if you go to Kingsville, Texas, home of the Kings Ranch, you'd notice the Spanish influences in language, religion, and architecture.

Dr. Crenshaw would tell the class about his work down at A&M-Kingsville. He stated that coming from the state of Missouri, and entering South Texas was an awaking that is indescribable. He noted that in his studies of the area and of the Hispanic culture, probably the most obvious aspect of cultural blending in the Valley was that of the local German and Irish communities with generations of Hispanics to form the Valley Texan. Dr. Crenshaw recalled stories of riding horseback at the Kings ranch, in the hot sun with his students looking for old markers left by earlier settlers. During his horse rides, he'd sing old cattle songs from Tex Ritters days, the cattle songs were very popular in the Rio Grande Valley.

A Valley Texan describes an individual with four or five generations dating back to the early Texas Immigrants into Mexico. Secondly, the Valley Texan grew up with a love for Country music favorites such as George Strait and Freddy Fender. Cowboy boots and jeans are the traditional wear for the area, and fajitas and BBQ can be eaten for almost any occasion.

In the DEEP, DEEP South, as they call it down in Alice, Texas, Mexico is considered a separate world. Some citizens is this neck of the world have never even seen the border—or anything outside of Three Rivers either! Some may ask, what is Mexico and who lives there.

To some, Mexico was the empire of the Aztec Indians, which controlled large areas of central and southern Mexico by the early 1500's. The Aztec capital was Tenochtitlan, one of the most important centers of trade and religion in the Americas, very similar to modern day Houston.

As a side note, Kathy and I took a trip to visit the pyramids when we were young. I heavily recommend a trip if you can and be sure to visit the museums. You will have the opportunity to view ancient art and see the secrets that the Aztec's kept for many centuries.

At the Pyramid of the Sun, we were walking down the side of one of the walkways. The tour guide was talking about the importance of religion and war and how they were focal points of Aztec society. Much of the Aztec's art, music, and poetry were intended to glorify their many gods. To remain in favor with their gods, the Aztecs practiced human sacrifice. They waged war almost constantly to obtain prisoners to be used as sacrifices.

Just imagine being a prisoner, and having to wait to be sacrificed. As usual Kathy decided to wait near a bench, and eat a large fried corn with butter, while I listened to the presentation regarding the governance of the culture. Kathy always loved to hear my side of the story, it made more sense then hearing it from the tour guide. I remember holding her hand and helping her up the tall pyramids. Kathy has a fear of heights, but that day, she trusted that I would not let her down. And I did promise to buy her another corn, to snack on. The guide continued, stating that in the Aztec society, laws were enforced by a system of courts, and criminals were often punished harshly for even small crimes. Aztecs encouraged their children to develop a sense of social responsibility from an early age. Children were required to attend school, where they prepared to become priests, warriors, craftsmen, or householders.

You must remember that it was an honor to be given up for sacrifice or to work in the temples. At this time, as Kathy was wrapping her snack up, I asked her if she'd consider it an honor to sacrificed (jokingly). She stated that, "Heck Tony, the high priest would probably need a team of horses and a band saw to get through me." Anyways, Kathy was pretty much done for tours that day. Latter on we went to the National Museum and attended classes and studied some more courses on Spanish government. Classes that I took during my years as a young student attending St. Philip Catholic School here in Dallas, the two years of theology at Bishop Lynch High School and a world history class with Coach Bundy left me with a clear understanding of the history of how Roman Catholic clergy introduced Spanish culture to the Indians. Some will state that religion was forced upon them against their will, but that's for the experts to debate. Father Eades would tell of how Priests and Friars started missions (missions are where they instructed the Indians in Spanish, Roman Catholicism, and various crafts).

Some missions did not succeed in molding the Indians to live and work in a European society. They did help start the process of mestizaje, the blending of Spanish and Indian cultures.

For example, he noted that Spanish priests used Christmas carols called villancicos and solemn pageants called posadas to teach the Indians about the events surrounding the birth of Jesus Christ.

Over the years, Indian composers wrote many villancicos about nonreligious subjects. Indians also turned the posadas into festive processions that took place in people's homes rather than in church.

I remember personally growing up and having my mother tell tales of the three kings and the sacred donkey that protected baby Jesus when he was asleep. It seems that while everyone was asleep, a simple donkey kept things from getting cold, by telling the other animals to breathe warm air on the site of baby Jesus. To this day, my mother will keep a small donkey in the house, named Reno. To serve as a reminder of the simple things, we take for granted.

Just like the tales of the sacred donkey that were past down from one generation to the next, art and the talents of Indian sculptors, craftsmen, and musicians were also pasted down. Indian wood and stone carvings decorated many buildings that otherwise were of traditional Spanish design.

The cathedral in San Luis Potasi is a marvel to be seen. I recommend touring the churches in Mexico, and examine the various artistic talents available. Musicians who combined the sounds of European and Indian instruments produced even new kinds of music. The Spaniards brought many technological improvements to Mexico. European farming methods and equipment generally brought better harvests than did Indian methods. On the other hand, for the cultivation of corn, the Spaniards did adopt Indian techniques. Thank heavens to the shared ideas that took place. Just imagine if the Spaniards had kept to themselves and discounted the advise of the natives. Corn probably would not have been as successful as it is throughout the world.

The intermixing of population groups took place in Mexico, as it did in the West Indies. But in Mexico, the intermingling occurred mainly among Spanish men and Indian women. The children of Spanish and Indian parentage became the mestizos, who today are the largest population group among Mexicans.

Hispanics in the United States share many of the traditional values claimed by most Americans. They place high value on their families and on success through hard work. They are also proud of their Latin-American heritage. Hispanics feel they should not lose contact with their cultures or their language. Instead, they seek to be bicultural and bilingual. Many hope that their cultures will someday be accepted as being part of American culture.

St. Patrick's Day is the perfect example of a holiday that everyone celebrates. It doesn't mean your Irish, but it means that you can share in some fun and another culture. Personally, I find it amusing that it's all right to waive Irish Flags, and sing, "Irish eyes are smiling" and drink a cold one. I enjoy the festivity and fellowship with some of my friends. But I realize that there are some in the community that get upset. Upset, should be reserved for those that don't enjoy life. Since, I enjoy life we should all be happy.

If you look at some of the courses offered in some private schools, you'll notice that learning one or more languages is not only beneficial but also economically advantageous. Imagine negotiating business deals and real estate transactions throughout the Southwest and even in parts of South America, without intercultural communications skills.

In the end it boils down to economics and business. Try going to Jesuit Prep, or St. Marks in Dallas and tell them that you have no desire to learn a second language, and they'll show you the door. Somewhere the idea of knowing just English became law. I find it funny that friends of mine in Europe can speak German, Spanish and a little French if they have to. My question is why does the public school system panic at secondary language learners. But private schools require it for graduation.

Another question that I'm asked most often is "Why don't Hispanics agree and act the same?" Well the answer is, there is no single Hispanic group and Hispanics do not act the same. A single Hispanic culture does not exist. Education, principle, and courage have a lot to say about group. I believe cultures have what is commonly known as subgroups within a micro group. For example, Education is a type of subgroup. Generally, professionals and those that attain a level of education form their own class group. Economic success is also a subgroup; sometimes association between the two groups is difficult. One group is considered mentally rich while the later may be financially rich but mentally poor.

The Micro groups share cultural traits, which cross-educational and financial borders. Food and economics are key weapons when it comes to negotiations. I believe that it was Ronald Reagan who stated that economics would always bridge any differences that a culture may have. Consider how economics played a role in the downfall of Communism in Russia. When my family began a campaign and sent over three thousand e-mails to the faithful asking them to pass it on to complained about the mini-series about President Reagan, economics kicked in and CBS pulled it from their program lineup.

The final weapon is food. Food is one area in which Hispanic influences are apparent in the United States. Mexican foods are especially popular. Taco Bell and Taco Bueno are probably the only examples that some people know of great Hispanic food.

Well I'm here to tell you that there's more to the taco then a folded tortilla filled with meat, cheese, and other ingredients. Today it is as common as hamburgers and hot dogs. The real heart of Mexican dishes, such as enchiladas, tamales, and tostadas, can be found in restaurants throughout the United States.

At the end of this book, I've included some of my mother's recipes from the old country. Her recipes date back to three or four generations. If you're not the cooking type, there are also some great restaurants in Dallas. One of my favorites is Ranchito's on Jefferson in Oak Cliff. It's rare to find a restaurant that doesn't hide behind others to make a good plate of enchiladas. I recommend dropping by and studying the history of Ranchito's.

You can always find Juan and Rubio dancing in the front door waiting to serve you. Always remember a good meal includes great music.

2

POLITICAL FLASHBACKS

UFW Founder Cesar Chavez & Linda Delgadillo

"When you do the common things in life in an uncommon way,
you will command the attention of the world."
George Washington Carver (1864–1943)

A lot of people in Texas have heard of the Flashback movement and others have not. To some it was an event that started the ball rolling. I coined the phrase because of the mixture of modern day activism and old country outreach. Flashback is simply a time that was frozen, and never again to be revisited.

Some of the leaders who helped in the organization of California grape pickers in 1962, included Cesar Chavez, Pancho Medrano, Hermelinda Delgadillo, John Zapata Gonzales, and Martin Morales.

I personally met these leaders. During the early 80's, we were all sitting in the old St. James cafeteria in Oak Cliff, eating and enjoying each other's company. Father Lucio, my family and Cesar were discussing life and the struggle. I find it odd that when he ate at our house and visited Dallas, people were embarrassed to be seen with him or even to march with him at a Safeway. The comments were, "He's some crazy man. Better stay away from him; he's nothing but trouble." I will never forget what he told me: "Antonio, in this world many people will claim to speak for others, but it takes an individual to represent beyond himself".

Since then I have been open-minded and have not let a lot get in the way of my philosophy. I remember Pancho Medrano and his son Robert who were big in my community while growing up. Since my family resided in the Edgemont district, Pancho was probably the only one not scared to come and visit our neighborhood. Our neighborhood, I'd like to say, was a flashback or at least its own world. Daily shootouts, drug dealing, and street violence were commonplace. Almost like a little Baghdad with daily shootings. Some of the toughest drug wars were fought in my two-block area. So in my view, anyone willing to come into my community had to be tough. Some will say that they were radicals or independent thinkers but I believe everyone should be able to dialogue with everyone. One common trait that you could say that we shared was toughness that some members in the Hispanic community in Dallas lack.

One event that made me realize that life is more then just a neighborhood or group was the era of thunder. The era of thunder was a time period during the late 70's and early 80's when our community was plagued with daily drug violence and killing. During some of the hottest days during the summer, the old west came alive on Ewing and Marsailas Streets. Rival gangs decided that they were tired of getting kicked around by the new Jamaican drug gangs coming in. Well, that summer the Cool Riders and Disciples met their match. Street thugs, pool hall pushers, small time thugs and members of "Old School" united for one final push. Armed with 38's and customized Chevy Nova's, they rolled into battle. Unfortunately, the only reminder of that night was the number of bullet holes in our roof from all the crossfire. It seems that everyone was just blasting and running in opposite directions.

My sister and I were on the second floor looking out the window with the lights off. Occasionally, a buzz would hit the side of the house, and you'd hear a thump on the wall. The sound is nothing like the movies, just allot of thumping. My mother must have been spread eagled on the floor. About two hours passed or so it seemed, when a police helicopter with a searchlight started looking for anyone that was still around. That night and for the next eight years, the Jamaicans ruled my neighborhood.

I'd have to say that after witnessing several gang fights, shootings, and rival drug factions kill off each other, our family could handle anything thrown at us.

You might begin to understand that the saying is true that leaders are not born, they're made. Just because you go to school and have the best of everything, it doesn't guarantee you 100% success. Life is a constant struggle, and will be until the day you die; some will complain and create excuses for their own failures in life. I've had cousins and friends go down needlessly, in gangs. Sometimes you fall, and I commend those that pick themselves up. But I'm honest enough to say that failure is internal not external. Society is simply an environment, which we live in; our inner selves dictate our decisions.

Let me repeat myself, society is where we live day to day. But the metal fabric of our soul keeps us going when hope and society give up on us. Simply put, failure by choice is another word for lack of guts.

I can say all this, because I've gone through it. You may disagree, or share a different view, but I believe it's the strength of moms everywhere that keep this nation going. This is especially true of the women of Texas, and probably the strongest leader I've known is my own mother.

I believe that history is made for those that write about it. Every individual has a story. But for the sake of history, I'm listing just a few that have played a role in the past and present. Hispanic leaders include such as crossover musicians Freddy Fender and Flaco Jimenez, NASA Astronaut Fernando "Frank" Caldeiro and comedian George Lopez.

University of Texas-Arlington professor Jose Angel Gutierrez, who helped establish La Raza Unida, a political party based in Texas, insists that his students must participate in a political function, regardless of party, to pass his class. He is preparing America's future electorate to take responsibility for the direction this country goes. That is true leadership.

Some will say that I am too conservative or too liberal, often reflecting their own bias. However, my response to them is, I am a Life member of the NRA,

TSRA, NAHA, and an advocate for the Arts. I support Adult and GED education, and believe in strong discipline in the schools. I support project EXILE, hunting, fishing, stock-car racing and boxing. I am not just a liberal or conservative—terms that are frequently used in an overly simplistic way to categorize. I am the son of an immigrant who played the cards dealt to him, a proud Texan and a patriotic American. Somehow, with all the different political ideology we still manage to continue. Discussion is good, without it we become stale or hollow in our thinking.

When individuals become stale and hollow they find themselves excluded from the political process. Voter apathy takes over and old ideas set the tone for the whole community.

Why is voter apathy dangerous? Voter apathy is to be considered like a dangerous cancer that is slowly draining life out of its victim. When Hispanics believe voting can't effectively change their lives, the social fabric of the entire community is weakened.

And when a community gives up, it impacts the economy. Currently, in Dallas and in other big cities, the poor leadership of the "OLD GUARD" has caused stagnation in this area. The "OLD GUARD" are those individuals that controlled the political realm in days gone by but have been unable to change with the tide. They hang on to past glories and do not realize that a new revolution is upon us.

"Driftwoods" are other individuals who claim to have all the questions and answers locked up. But in reality they have lost touch with the current political environment. They may have had answers in the past but they cannot come up with new answers to meet today's challenges.

Beware of the OLD GUARD and Driftwoods, who work hand-in-hand with each other, because just as fast as they speak they're sticking you in the back with gossip and rumors. You ask yourself, why doesn't anyone dialog or how does a city simply stay quiet? Well the answer is simple; if you want a solution, develop one! If your looking to stall for more time and don't really need a solution, form a committee. Add some Driftwoods and OLD GUARD and you're sure to have a good ole' Texas Mud Fight. Just for entertainment, count how many times they call each other sellouts. Its funny to watch them wrap themselves in the Flag, when the money they take under the table is not green but blood red. We all know who they are, they have been in Dallas and North Texas for years. They serve as Hispanic Consultants and sit on committees and do absolutely nothing to aide their candidate or assist in the community.

To survive in the new America, groups of yester-year need to identify with the new Hispanics coming in. Only those individuals willing to listen and work with first or second generation Hispanics can have a chance at success in the new century.

3

ERA OF THE "DEAD HORSE"

Tony & State Rep. Fred Hill

"A people that values its privileges above its principles soon loses both."
Dwight D. Eisenhower (1890–1969)

Dwight D. Eisenhower said it best that a people that values it privileges above its principles soon loses both. The values of Hispanics are strong and made of solid steel. But just as solid steel rusts with time, values gone unchecked will also rust.

The days of forming committees and doing nothing will slowly fade into periods of stagnation. Hispanics are among the fastest-growing U.S. groups. But their political influence has increased at a much slower pace. Fundamentally, this is due to the lack of leadership.

Since the 1990's, Hispanic attitudes toward politics have changed. Voter registration drives have added hundreds of Hispanics to the rolls. That's right, hundreds—because when you register one group, twice the number registering is released from the rolls for failing to vote. Some groups pretend to represent past causes, and it is their failure that requires them to shut up and learn from the new groups coming into town.

You've heard me discuss the phrase of Dead Horses. Well down in the country an old wise professor once told me a strong horse will run, work and is capable of doing anything without question. And as the horse ages, it begins to realize that its days of usefulness are coming to an end. You'll notice a lone horse out in a field looking out as if it was watching a herd of cattle. The owner, if he's not careful, will assume that the horse is simply being stubborn, and force him to work more. Then one day the horse will walk off, and lay down somewhere deep in the woods, so that the owner cannot find him and live out his last days sleeping, preparing for his travel to the next life. And if the owner finds the horse, it is practically impossible to get the horse up or move him. This is because the horse has given up on life, and by all laws of nature, did what he could.

The reverse is true for humans! Some leaders, don't know how and where to get out to pasture, even business leaders who are comfortable with the status quo will revitalize the Dead Horse. Which in the end forms the bulk of the Driftwoods.

Driftwoods love lawsuits because they stall things for a while, due to the surplus of dead horses that have plagued the Hispanic community. Time and time again it has been shown through the federal courts that voting district boundaries had been purposely drawn to split Hispanic communities putting liberal with conservative and vise versa. The courts have ordered district lines to be redrawn to better represent established communities. With the new boundaries in place, more candidates supported by Hispanics have been elected to office. But due to the "Dead Horse Theory", candidates have risen to the top of already shaky structures.

All too often they have amounted to spineless mouthpieces for outworn ideas. They bark a lot and scream injustice, but when a fight gets started they are the first to run and the last to take a stand on anything. I can just see them in a beer commercial saying "Less filling or does it taste great or is it filling and tastes great". Generally, you can always count on their cowardliness to keep them quiet.

History has shown that during the 80's, there were just six Hispanic Americans serving in the U.S. Congress. By the mid-90's, that number had increased to 20. On the national scene, other elected officials included former Miami mayor Maurice Ferre, the first Hispanic mayor of a large U.S. city and Xavier Suarez, Miami's first Cuban born mayor.

My sister Kathy noted that this was the greatest day in Miami—it was like the Super Bowl and a major Hurricane party rolled into one. As a side note, Kathy (also referred to as Katherine in this book) took active steps in the state of Florida. She attended Barry University and was very active in politics and other civic duties. My sister stated, "In Miami, there are two voices, one that talks and one that yells!" Most of you can tell that when something needs to get done, she's way ahead of the game. Katherine loves working in campaigns, quietly and swiftly she'll work to ensure victory. Each election our entire family will work on a strategy that will ensure a very interesting outcome for the candidate. Think of us as the "Mind Benders".

Kathy cites individuals that come out on top due to their struggle and determination is amazing. One of her favorite role models was also a short tough kid who came from a large family. "AL" Gonzales, legal aide to President George W. Bush, when he was the Texas governor, was dedicated to his job.

Personally, my award for struggle would have to go to Tony Garza. The former Railroad Commissioner to Texas who is currently serving as Ambassador to Mexico. When he first ran for office he struggled and overcame his Democrat district by reaching beyond party lines and seeing the people for who they are. "PEOPLE". Sometimes politicians or leaders forget who they represent, and end up working for the wrong group and fail in their mission. One woman that stays reserved but works behind the scenes is really a hard working representative.

State Rep. Elvira Reyna, out of District 101, was the first elected Hispanic female from North Texas. One day I was walking out of a dinner reception that she had hosted for a fundraiser, and from that day, I knew she was all right. All right in a sense that she believed in what she was doing, despite the lack of support from some "Old Guards" or the fact that she was a woman. You'd be surprised at the impressions that go around about female politicians. Personally, I'm glad that she's stayed around and broke through and served. One day, as each of the DRIFTWOODS pass away, I see a bright future for her. After she leaves the state house this year, it will be a new beginning for a strong leader.

Even with these gains, however, Hispanic Americans still accounted for less than 2 percent of U.S. elected officials in the late 1990's.

During the mid 80's, I can remember President Reagan reaching out to the Cuban community and Hispanic community, especially here in Dallas. During the Republican National Convention, my dear friend John Z. Gonzales was sitting in the front row and Reagan acknowledge his help in the promotion of America.

Even today while drinking coffee, John and I will talk about politics and the changing scene here in the United States.

Everyone knows that John was a U.S. Marine in Korea. Attached to the 1st Marine Division, Fleet Marine Forces, John defended freedom, earned the Purple Heart and came back to the United States to work in the community. His son Michael still runs the Bilingual Yellow Pages here in Dallas.

Another standout was Lauro Cavazos, who became the first Hispanic cabinet member when President Ronald Reagan appointed him Secretary of Education. President George H.W. Bush kept Cavazos in this post, where he remained until 1990.

Other presidential appointments since 1980, include Katherine Ortega, U.S. Treasurer under Reagan; Manuel Lujan, Jr., Interior Secretary under Bush; Antonia C. Novello became the nation's first Hispanic Surgeon General. These successes are mere examples and as reflected in earlier chapters, the list could go on and on.

4

BIRTH OF THE TEJANO

"The man who goes alone can start today; but he who travels
with another must wait till that other is ready."
by: Henry David Thoreau 1817–62

Chapter four birth of the Tejano, explains itself. Richard Morales offered some insight and thoughts from his experience researching the topic. To this day, Richard is seen running the libraries updating his research. Along with some thoughts this chapter will open the foundation, upon which we lay the bricks and mortar of the modern day Tejano. One must remember that Tejanos originate from Texas, and their history is uniquely different from other states in the southwest. So instead of reinventing the wheel, I'd like to credit Dr. Andres Tijerina. Some of the original text has been inserted, and left unchanged. This allows for the flow to continue and research the terms you may notice and wish to independently research on your own.

You may notice some input from myself, here and there, but after this chapter I'll explain other issues regarding differences in the Hispanic Culture.

Sometimes when I talk to various groups, some listeners ask questions and I answer with the best information that I can find. Sometimes when you read the history, you'd be surprised at the similarities with other cultures.

This article focuses on Texas between 1821 and 1836 in an effort to provide structure for an understanding of the exchange of land, power, culture, and social institutions that took place during those critical years. To understand Tejano origins in this period, it is necessary to review Tejano society and local government in the municipalities of Texas and the legacy of the Hispanic frontera concept. It is necessary to consider the evolution of the statehood of Texas under the Mexican republic and the legacy of Tejano statesmen. These were the people who wrote the laws, which defined Tejano life and invited Anglo immigration. Tejano life under the Mexican flag is what made Texas so uniquely a part of the Hispanic tradition.

Spanish colonial administrators had originally settled Texas as a "buffer province" for northern New Spain. The Spaniards had learned from the Iberian Peninsula centuries earlier to use a buffer zone between their own settlements and those of the Moorish invaders. They had learned to control a depopulated zone, or despoblado, for defensive purposes as they steadily conquered their lands from the Moors. The Spaniards had established armed municipalities, presidios or forts, and missions within the despoblado. These municipalities, presidios, and missions constituted the defensive borderland or frontera.

A second factor unifying the Tejano frontera was the mixture of the racial groups peculiar to Tejano settlements. Soldiers stationed on the frontera integrated socially into the Tejano civilian communities, reinforcing the unity of the different regions. And finally, the racial heritage of the Tejanos reinforced the contrast between them and the Anglo-American settlers daily arriving from the

United States. Indeed, in its very settlement, Texas had developed a defensive governmental structure, which was described by historian Herbert E. Bolton as being almost wholly military.

In 1718, the Presidio de San Antonio de Bear and the Mission San Antonio de Valero were established in Béxar on the San Antonio. The founders later established the missions of San José, San Juan, Concepción, and San Francisco de Espada. The Béxar population fluctuated between roughly 1,500 and 2,000 throughout the years 1805 to 1833. Further down the San Antonio River from Béxar, near the Gulf coast was Goliad. The Goliad community was very similar to Béxar, particularly in the founding of the Presidio La Bahía del Espíritu Santo and blending into the surrounding community. La Bahía appeared more dynamic than Béxar in many ways. Ironically, La Bahía had not become an official villa until 1820. Its population, which was in the villa surrounding the presidio and on neighboring ranches, had traditionally been about half that of Béxar. But within a few years, the population of the area began an upward trend. During this time, La Bahía changed its name to Goliad. Also at this time, Goliad was joined by the new settlement of Guadalupe de Jesús Victoria, which was founded nearby.

The Goliad presidiales contributed greatly to the population, and more significantly, they provided outstanding leadership among the Tejano community in general. Indeed, a steady flow of distinguished Goliad citizens emanated from the presidio. These included Carlos de la Garza of the well-known "Carlos Rancho" and Ignacio Zaragoza, who went on to become the victorious general at the famous Mexican battle of the "Cinco de Mayo." Another very important Tejano, though seldom recognized in history, was the former commander of the presidio, Rafael Antonio Manchola. Manchola became one of the most successful Tejano statesmen in Coahuila y Texas politics. He had arrived at La Bahía in 1822, served as a state congressman, and became the Goliad ayuntamiento president in 1831. Likewise, Captain Jose de Jesus Aldrete had retired as the presidio commander, and established a ranch in 1821 near the presidio. The Aldrete family later went on to settle in a new village known as San Patricio.

When the first settlers arrived in 1821, Tejano settlement consisted of three distinct and separate regions—the Nacogdoches region, the Béxar-Goliad region along the San Antonio River, and the Río Grande ranching frontier between the Nueces River and the Río Grande. Each of these populations fluctuated independently from the others; and yet, all of them shared certain characteristics in common. The basic factor unifying the Tejano community was the military purpose of the settlements.

All Tejanos shared a military background, which had developed into a strong sense of mission to defend Mexico's northern frontera. Ranches represented a significant social element in the Béxar-Goliad region. A belt of ranches extended along much of the San Antonio River between Béxar and Goliad. The ranchero move onto ranches indicates the Tejano value for the land and ranching lifestyle as opposed to living in town. (As a side note while researching this chapter and focusing on the earlier history, I was able to drive down to La Bahia and Goliad. Let me tell you, the history just jumps out at you. If you are interested, take I-35 south and continue till you hit San Antonio and then take 37 towards Corpus Christi. The little towns from Kennedy to Gonzales still have the feel of the settlers from that time. It is hard to believe that Texas was originally the wasteland of the North. Secondly, if you go to Fannin, I recommend eating the barbeque and visiting the town center. Anna even fired a small mission cannon in the old fort La Bahia.)

The northern region of Tejano settlements in this period was Nacogdoches. Removed in physical distance from the Béxar-Goliad region, Nacogdoches was also distinct in character. Unlike Béxar, Nacogdoches had no major presidio to feed its bloodlines. Instead, the Nacogdoches racial and cultural structure drew as much from its French and Anglo neighbors in Louisiana as it did from Mexico far to the south. Located on a well-established trade route between Mexico and the United States, Nacogdoches lacked the comfortable inertia of Bexareño society. And Nacogdoches developed more than any other Tejano settlement the ability to remove its entire populace in time of attack and return when conditions permitted. Throughout its existence, the population of Nacogdoches ebbed and flowed, evacuated but never abandoned its frontier homeland.

To the south of the original Tejano settlements lived a third population, which at the turn of the century was just on the threshold of an upward thrust from the Río Grande toward the Nueces. Formerly citizens of Tamaulipas and northern Mexico, these southern rancheros became citizens of Texas by virtue of the boundary claims by Texas to the Río Grande after the Texas Revolution. More significantly, they became Tejanos by settling lands under the new head right programs of the Republic of Texas. With these head right settlers came a wave of other immigrants from Mexico. All of these people, strongly Mexican, probably thought of themselves as "Mexicans" rather than as "Texans." Nevertheless, they were closer to the Béxar-Goliad region than Nacogdoches was. All three groups had descended from the same families and bloodlines. And in any case, they all stood across the same cultural and racial lines from the Anglo-Texans after 1836.

By 1835, approximately 350 ranches existed in this region, many of which provided the foundation for future Texas towns. The major ranches included San Diego, San Juan, Palo Blanco, Agua Dulce, El Sauz, Los Olmos, San Luis, Pansacol, Zapata, San Ignacio, and Los Saenz.

One of the first major events to affect Texas in the nineteenth century occurred when it was still a province of Mexico, or New Spain. In September 1810, New Spain felt the first tremors of a movement for freedom when a Mexican priest named Miguel Hidalgo began a movement, which would lead to independence from Spain. As a result of the independence movement, Texas obtained its own provincial deputation, which governed it until the promulgation of the federal constitution of 1824. This new constitution ended Texas' experiment as a self-governed province by making it a department of the new state of Coahuila y Texas. One of the most important facets of Tejano life was the Mexican form of local government, which prevailed in the years between the consummation of Mexican independence in 1821, and the Texan Revolution in 1836. That government was an essential part of Tejano life because, based as it was in the Roman tradition, it set forth a "code" for society. From this code emerged the basic political principles to which the Tejano strove to adhere in the daily governance of their community. A survey of Tejano government then provides not only a study of that political philosophy, but a structural framework of Tejano life as well.

The basic unit of Mexican government was the municipality. The jurisdiction of the municipio, as it was called, encompassed the city. But unlike a modern city, the municipality jurisdiction included the surrounding area as well, not unlike a modern American county. According to the dictates of the Spanish codes of the Recopilación, a Spanish municipality should be governed by an ayuntamiento or city council, comprised of its own citizens. After allowing for the establishment of ayuntamientos in the older municipalities, the state government of Coahuila y Texas decreed in June 1827, that each ayuntamiento should draw up and submit its municipal ordinances for approval in Saltillo. By 1834, all of the old Tejano municipalities had established a formal government. Each had a constitutional alcalde and the specified number of regidores. And each municipality laid out its own town plat, which was actually a square. The principal town square or plaza was in the center with perpendicular streets oriented to the four ordinal directions. Each city street as well as the plaza itself was set to standard measurements, so many varas or yards (approximately) in length and width. The east side of the plaza was designated for ecclesiastical structures such as the cathedral, the chapel, or the chancery. On the west side were the government and public buildings such as the casa capitular or state house, the customs house, and the governor's palace.

The single most distinguishing characteristic of Tejano culture was the strong sense of community. The early Spaniards had brought with them a strong neighborhood concept of the barrio, which was reinforced, on the Texas frontera. Then as the early expeditions came in to settle Texas, the people came as whole families or communities. Some of these families grouped themselves around the early missions where they remained for decades. Others huddled around the presidio or in distant communities like Nacogdoches, where even the different races tended to be drawn together. To the nineteenth-century Tejano, the barrio was home, and the vecindario, or neighboring populace, was family. It was not enough for municipal government to provide an alcalde as the leader of the town. Each barrio had to have its own resident comisario or "judge of the barrio." The comisarios, who saw to the social welfare and administrative matters in their respective barrios, were seen officially as the heads of these extended families. One Béxar ordinance described the comisarios as "the true Fathers of the vecindario in their respective territories".

Standard procedure in the management of a municipality's social functions called for the appointment of quasi-official committees, or municipal commissions. These commissions were composed of local government officials, professionals in the respective endeavor, and ordinary citizens. They were responsible for collecting funds, making necessary arrangements, and conducting the operations of the social function. One such municipal commission was the *Junta* Patriotica, or the Patriotic Committee. It was responsible for the operation of patriotic or civic endeavors. Their most common activities involved official celebrations, however, of such events as Constitution Day, the Feast of Corpus Christi, Christmas, Good Thursday and Friday, the Feast of San Felipe de Jesús, the Feast of the Virgin of Guadalupe, and Independence Day. Preparations for these events sent the city official busily buying the refreshments, renting a dance hall, and contracting for the musicians.

Mexican Independence Day was one of the major themes of the year. By 1825, it had been officially ordered that the 16th of September would be a national feast of "the first grito [proclamation] of independence." This celebration was a highlight of the year for Tejanos. The festivities involved a three-day celebration starting on September 15 with a torchlight parade, a cannonade and the ringing of church bells. The next day began with a solemn Te Deum mass, a day parade, speeches, and the official reenactment of the grito. Prisoners were released, troops paraded, and señoritas were officially invited to the gran baile or grand ball, sometimes called a fandango. At the fandango, a señorita Tejana could dance and display her fine dress. The Tejana wore one of the most distinctive, though seldom recognized of Mexico's regional costumes. The formal announcement to the fandango was a colorful affair, much like a parade, called a convite or invitation. The young men of the city rode in a group on gaily decorated horses through the streets, playing the guitar and singing as they went. The third day terminated the activities with all the citizens dressed in mourning to attend a "mass for the departed." Throughout all of these activities, the *Junta Patriotica* was responsible for refreshments, music, and official speeches.

Tejano water law also amply illustrates the Tejanos' development of local self-government. Their Hispanic background had given the Tejanos a highly developed philosophy on water management. Drawing on this tradition, the Tejanos created local water systems, which they governed, by basic principles of ancient law. In so doing, the Tejanos instituted the first adaptation of European civilization to the semiarid environment of Texas. More than a century later, the Anglo would add the advantages of technology to the acquisition and control of water. The result was a combination, which would become one of the many distinctive traits of Texas. In fact, few institutions demonstrate as vividly as water law the historical genius of Texas for combining Mexican traditional culture with Anglo technology.

Tejano water systems included the land units along the rivers called porciones, which were elongated land tracts. They included the dams, the irrigation canals or acequias, the aqueducts, and fields—many of which still carry water today. The influence of Hispanic water philosophy is fairly common in modern Texas, where vocabulary as well as law books include such words as suerte, porción, acequia, surco, agastodero, labor, arroyo, and canoa.

Education was another major area of concern to the Tejano community. No other facet of life was so exclusively dependent on local support. Through their local Public Education Commission or the Comisión de Escuelas, Tejanos continually strived to erect a viable education system. Their objectives guided the educational efforts of later Tejano generations; and their ideals created a prototype for the successful system, which Texas boasts today.

Each municipality hired its own schoolteachers. Béxar hired José Antonio Gama y Fonseca, Victoriano Zepeda, and Bruno Huizar. Goliad had a small school, which served intermittently until 1821, employing soldiers from the presidio. Laredo established its school in 1825 when it hired Juan José Salinas as the teacher for twenty pesos per month from local contributors. One of the commendable efforts was that of Nacogdoches. In 1828, the Junta Piadosa began a determined effort in the community and in the state legislature to establish a school.

Their proposals stimulated the legislature to initiate a new program of land grants for education. In fact, free education was one of the major provisions of a Tejano school ordinance entitled "Ordinance Which Shall Be Observed in the Public Free Primary School Dedicated to the Instruction of the Youth of the Vicinity of Béxar." But while Tejanos strived to stabilize life in their villas, they also had to provide for law and order for the surrounding ranchland as well.

The nature of the despoblado only compounded the challenge of life on the frontera. This hinterland held valuable resources, some of which were peculiar to Texas. To exploit these, Tejanos employed the Hispanic institution of the rancho. Indeed, some historians have viewed ranching as one of the most significant institutions on the Mexican frontier. No other place in the world had as many wild longhorn or as many mustangs as South Texas by the mid-eighteenth century. Indeed, mesteña is a uniquely Tejano word in the Spanish and Mexican dictionaries. The Tejano perfected horsemanship along with the branding, the round-ups, the cattle drives, and all the other aspects, which have become hallmarks of ranching in the United States today.

In their efforts to incorporate the despoblado economically, however, the Tejanos confronted all of its hostile elements. Tejanos therefore had to extend their authority outward from the municipality and onto the despoblado. By incorporating it, Tejanos tended then to combine their livelihood with their defense. Thus, as they extended the ranch into the Texas despoblado, Tejanos provided for the emergence of a rural policeman. This policeman had the authority of a rural judge. He was called the Juez de Campo. In all of its uniquely Mexican forms, this institution was to survive with ranching as an archetype in the defense of the Texas backcountry. The Juez de Campo served to register the brands, regulate the sale of cattle, and to arbitrate disputes among the ranchers. And in his pursuit of cattle rustlers, the Juez de Campo, Tejanos played a major role in developing a unique frontier defense unit called a compañía volante or cavalry flying squadron.

Tejanos acquired their special knowledge of offensive cavalry tactics from the military squadrons of the frontera. The most important of these units was the compañía volante. This unique type of military squadron structure was perfected during the liberalization of the independence years in Mexico. Tejano flying squadrons developed to the authority for extended pursuit and the authority to enlist the aid of *comisarios*, or to deputize citizens. Effective long-range pursuit was essential on the Texas *despoblado*, and it was a common method used by

Tejanos. Their skill with horses lent them a natural mobility. Their experience with Indians and their knowledge of the *despoblado* made them formidable stalkers and scouts. And finally, their military ancestry and background had nurtured in them a familiarity with military organization, cavalry tactics, and particularly, a predilection for the offensive campaign.

Undoubtedly the flying squadron had extraordinary effectiveness on the despoblado in the nineteenth century. It effectively combined the principles of mobility, incessant pursuit, and the advantages of an offensive frontier guard. Considering the characteristics—good and bad—of the Rangers in mid-nineteenth-century South Texas, it appears that the Texas Rangers could well have represented something of a connecting link between the Tejano flying squadrons of the 1830s and the Rurales of the 1890s.

As Tejanos adjusted to their status as a department of Coahuila y Texas, they participated in writing the colonization laws that invited Anglo-Americans into Texas, and they committed themselves to an unfavorable status in Mexico. As Coahuiltejanos, they saw their prosperity in the success of Anglo-American colonization. In support of this colonization, they formed a legislative policy, which was at the vanguard of liberal thought in Mexico of the 1830s. Indeed, they established in this effort some of the most beneficial legal institutions of their cultural legacy for Texas and the United States, such as their law, which became the model for the American Homestead Law. But, their protective attitude toward Anglo-Americans led Tejanos into direct conflict with the more conservative centralists of Mexico and eventually alienated them from the growing centralist government in Mexico City.

But even as Tejanos began to conflict with the Centralist government in Mexico, they began to conflict with their new Anglo neighbors as well. For years Tejanos alone had resisted the intrusions of Anglo-American adventurers. Their supportive attitude toward colonization struggled against a strong cultural bias, which made them perceive many Anglos as crude and asocial. Tejanos thus increasingly defined themselves as an entity different from Mexico and separate from the Anglo. Although Santa Anna and the Anglo-Americans in the Texas Revolution have held center stage in the story of Texas, Tejano politics was as much a factor as Mexican centralism or Anglo rebellion in determining the course of Tejanos and Texas.

By the time their state constitution was promulgated in 1827, the Tejanos and other liberal Coahuiltejanos had committed themselves to achieving economic prosperity through their state colonization program. Tejanos collaborated with a liberal group of thinkers who were the statesmen from Parras and Monclova. José

María Viesca and his brother Agustín led the group in political ideology and power. Both served in national positions as well as state. They were intellectuals who promoted liberal political and scientific thought, and their family was known in Mexico as very liberal. Their family was described as "rich, large, respectable, learned, sensible, and honorable.

One of the strongest motives which *Coahuiltejanos* had in supporting economic enterprise, self-interest, is most evident in their efforts to sponsor the cotton industry and to attract U.S. cotton planters to Texas. In this effort, the Tejanos sponsored pro-slavery measures to induce Anglo-American immigration, and similarly established a program of land laws as a foundation for settlement and prosperity. Some, such as the homestead protection, were developed explicitly to attract southern U.S. debtors. Many of their laws were based upon ancient Hispanic tradition; others were imaginative answers to frontier imperative.

Almost all of them were continued under different titles by Anglo-Americans in Texas and the United States after 1836 as the Headright Land Grants of the Republic of Texas and the Pre-Emption Land Law.

Another Coahuiltejano law, issued as Decree No. 95 on July 3, 1829, granted the state the right to establish its own territorial limits. This law became particularly important to Texas when oil was discovered in the Gulf of Mexico near the Texas coast. Thus through the implementation and development of ancient Hispanic land policies, Coahuiltejanos provided a major impetus in drawing the Anglo-American tide southward to Texas.

Nevertheless, Tejanos at this time also began to conflict with their new Anglo neighbors. In one early incident, a tense situation between DeWitt's colony and the Tejanos erupted into open conflict within a year of DeWitt's arrival. In March 1826, the Tejano leader and empresario, Martín de Leon, sued an Anglo colonist in a dispute over livestock. And in October, De Leon went to confiscate some contraband goods, which Anglo colonists had hidden in DeWitt's colony. Indeed, the commander of La Bahía Presidio, Rafael Antonio Manchola, escorted De Leon with an armed troop. When the colonists heard that the Tejanos were coming and that De Leon had sworn to return with DeWitt's head, the Anglo-Americans armed themselves for resistance. An armed conflict was averted, but the incident was only the beginning of a long series of conflicts between the Anglos and Tejanos for years to come.

Tejanos were very much aware of the widening cultural gap between them and the rest of Mexico as well. As the political situation worsened after the Law of April 6, 1830, Tejanos in Bexar, Nacogdoches and Goliad drew up memorials in 1833. The Goliad memorial is perhaps the most revealing of Tejano sentiments at the time. It began with a declaration of the social contract and ended with a threat of secession by the same sanction.

> "If the people who are ruled by despots are permitted the natural right of revolutionary measures against their oppression then those people, who by their own consent live under the divine republican system, have also had conceded to them by the political compact the right to petition as a primary measure which they may use toward remedying the evils which afflict them, whether those evils originate from the inertia of the laws, by the ignorance of the Legislators, or by the ineptitude of their governing officials."

In a classic Mexican phrase of protest, the Goliad leaders exhorted "Basta ya." [Enough] The allusion to "ignorant" legislators was certainly not lost on Santa Anna. Unfortunately, however, as Tejanos protested through the chain of command within the Mexican government, Anglos under new leaders from the United States took matters into their own hands, and worked independently from Tejanos. Texas finally arose in arms, but the people of Texas stood in separate camps. With the fall of the Alamo and Goliad to Santa Anna's forces in 1836, the Tejano experiment with liberal legislation was forever at an end.

If life had been difficult for Tejanos before the coming of the Anglo-Americans, it was even more so after 1836. In 1836, Tejanos discovered that Mexican centralists presented just as much a threat to Tejano security as foreign enemies. They realized that the Texas frontera was not simply a frontier boundary or buffer zone, but a separate entity between two frontiers. The Texas Revolution and the Mexican War brought years of turmoil for Texas and for Tejanos. The Tejanos, who could claim Texas in 1820, had lost that claim by 1836. The Anglo-American population poured into Texas after the revolution, making the Tejanos a distinct minority in their native land. Tejanos remained in large enough numbers, of course, to provide a degree of continuity of their Mexican culture in Texas. Those who had held their ground during the revolution and those who returned afterward continued the process of cultural transmission to the incoming order.

The most traumatic effects of the revolution were the initial wave of racial conflict and the resulting land exchange between Anglo and Tejano. At first, men fought for political principle, but soon political principle became racial polarization as well. Tejanos quickly were forced to choose sides. Those who did not voluntarily side with Mexico were either forced to do so, or were subjected to harassment. Tejano leaders like Juan N. Seguin and Fernando de Leon of Victoria were harassed by Mexican Centralists and by Anglos as well. The entire town of Goliad was stripped of its arms and its Tejano leaders physically abused by a Mexican general in 1835. When the Texas army arrived there a year later, Anglo troops crashed, robbed, and plundered the homes, driving Tejano families out. Similar conditions prevailed at Nacogdoches where Tejano families were continually robbed of their livestock, grain, and belongings. Many Tejanos such as Carlos de la Garza, Vicente Cordova, and eventually Juan N. Seguin turned against the militant Anglos. Hundreds of Tejano families, however, scattered onto the ranches and eventually into Coahuila and Tamaulipas. Enough Tejano families remained throughout the wars, however, and many were able to regain their lands, and even to become competitive ranchers and merchants after the Mexican War, particularly in the region south of the Nueces River.

There the campaigns of the Mexican War actually spurred the population growth along the Río Grande. The most immediate effects of General Taylor's occupation, for example, was to stimulate trade and introduce some semblance of order-albeit military-to the region. Even as the war raged in Central Mexico, the modern towns of the Río Grande region were being born. From the old ranches eventually grew the new American towns of Corpus Christi, Eagle Pass, Brownsville, Edinburgh, and Río Grande City. The San Patricio land district of Texas was finally organized into several new counties. An American diocese was created, an official census was taken, and American city governments were organized with new government officials, including some old ranchero patriarchs. By 1848, the number of Tejanos was in an upward swing, led particularly by the robust ranch frontier of the Río Grande.

The distinctiveness of Tejano culture is in its combination of conflict and heritage. Conflict inhered in Tejano life on the frontera. From their first settlement on the Texas frontera to the post-revolutionary decades of unrest, Tejanos knew conflict in their daily lives. Defense had become a part of their unique culture. Their heritage was more than simply Mexican. It was a Mexican heritage, which retained significant aspects of Indian and Spanish culture and developed under constant conditions of conflict.

The story of the Tejano culture is definitely not one of decline. The Tejano population dwindled in relation to the flood of Anglo-Americans who poured into Texas, but the Tejanos and their families remained in the Texas Republic. In fact, the strongest surge that Tejano population experienced was between San Antonio and the Río Grande after 1836. More significantly, the Tejano culture has been adopted and spread by the Anglo-Americans themselves. Because Texas was the first Mexican state settled by the Anglo-American tide, Texas probably had a greater influence initially on that westward-moving frontier. The use of words like lasso, corral, and mustang in distant western states like Wyoming and Montana indicate the extent to which the tools, techniques, and animals of the Tejanos have spread across the United States. With those tools and animals, of course, spread the laws for water, land, and resource management. Aspects of Tejano life have colored and benefited American life. The tremendous herds of Tejano cattle provided beef for a steak-and-hamburger-eating nation in its dynamic industrialization phase. And Tejano laws laid much of the foundation for a prosperous Texan society. Indeed, the history of Texas can never be complete without the story of her original founders—the Tejanos.

People of Mexican descent in Texas trace their biological origins to the racial mixture that occurred following the Spanish conquest of Mexico in the 1520s. During the Spanish colonial period, population increases occurred as Spanish males mixed with Indian females, begetting a mestizo race. By 1821, when Mexico won its independence from Spain, the mestizo population almost equaled the size of the indigenous stock and that of Iberian born persons. Mexicans advanced northward from central Mexico in exploratory and settlement operations soon after the conquest, but did not permanently claim the Texas frontier land until after 1710. In the late seventeenth and early eighteenth centuries, the French became increasingly active along the Texas Gulf Coast, and in response, the viceroy in Mexico City made preparations for the colonization of the Texas wilderness.

The first expedition in 1716 peopled an area that subsequently became the town of Nacogdoches; a second in 1718 settled present-day San Antonio; and a third established La Bahía (Goliad) in 1721. During the 1740s and 1750s, the crown founded further colonies along both banks of the Rio Grande, including what is now Laredo. At this early time, the crown relied primarily on persuasion to get settlers to pick up and relocate in the far-off Texas lands. Those responding hailed from Coahuila and Nuevo León, though intrepid souls from the interior joined the early migrations. In reality, few pioneers wished to live in isolation or amid conditions that included possible Indian attack. They feared a setting that lacked adequate supplies, sustenance, and medical facilities for the sick, especially infants.

The total Mexican descent population in Texas may have approximated 700,000 by 1930. The Great Depression and repatriation efforts and deportation drives undertaken during the 1930s stymied population expansion. Growth resumed during the 1940s, however, as labor shortages in the United States induced common people from Mexico to seek escape from nagging poverty in the homeland. Many turned to Texas ranches and farms, but also to urban opportunities, as the state entered the post-World War II industrial boom. Their presence, combined with births among the native-born population, augmented the Spanish-surnamed population to 1,400,000 by 1960. Though economic refugees from Mexico continued to add to the expansion of Tejano communities after the 1960s, the majority of children born since that date have had native-born parents. The 1990 census counted 4,000,000 people of Mexican descent in the state. Less than 20 percent of that population was of foreign birth.

The rise of commercial agriculture in the late nineteenth and early twentieth centuries summoned laborers for seasonal and farm work, and both recent arrivals from Mexico and native-born Tejanos answered the call by heading into South and Central Texas fields. During this period, they also made for Southeast Texas and North Texas, searching out cotton lands as well as opportunities in large cities such as Houston and Dallas. Between 1910 and 1929, migrant workers began what became a yearly migrant swing that started in the farms of South Texas and headed northward into the developing Northwest Texas and Panhandle cotton lands. They settled in smaller communities along the routes of migration, and by the 1930s the basic contours of modern-day Tejano demography had taken form. With the exception of Northeast Texas, most cities and towns in the state by the pre-World War II era had Tejano populations. Tejanos relied on a wide spectrum of occupations in the nineteenth century, though most found them confined to jobs as day laborers and in other unspecialized tasks.

They worked as maids, restaurant helpers, and laundry workers, but the great majority turned to range duties due to the orientation of the economy and their skills as ranch hands and shepherds. A small percentage found a niche as entrepreneurs or ranchers. After the 1880s, Texas Mexicans turned to new avenues of livelihood, such as building railroads and performing other arduous tasks. During the agricultural revolution of the late nineteenth and the early twentieth centuries, many worked grubbing brush and picking cotton, vegetables, and fruits, primarily in the fields of South Texas, but also migrated into the other regions of the state as farmhands.

In the urban settlements, an entrepreneurial sector-comprising shop owners, labor agents, barbers, theater owners, restaurateurs, and the like-ministered to Mexican consumers in familiar terms. Even as Texas society experienced increased urban movements following World War I, Tejanos remained preponderantly an agrarian people.

In towns, many faced labor segregation and took menial jobs in construction work, city projects, railroad lines, slaughterhouses, cotton compresses, and whatever else availed itself. After World War II, however, increased numbers of

Tejanos left agricultural work and found opportunities in the industrializing cities. Most found improvements in wages and working conditions in unskilled or semiskilled positions, though a growing number penetrated the professional, managerial, sales, clerical, and craft categories.

Presently, the great majority of Tejanos hold urban-based occupations that range from high paying professional positions to minimum wage, unskilled jobs. An unfortunate minority remains tied to farm work as migrating campesinos.

Since the initial settlements of the early eighteenth century, a sense of community has given Tejanos a particular identity. On the frontier, common experiences and problems forced Texas Mexicans to adjust in ways different from those of their counterparts in the Mexican interior. Tejanos fashioned an ethic of self-reliance, wresting their living from a ranching culture, improvising ways to survive in the wilderness expanse, and devising specific political responses to local needs despite directives from the royal government. In barrios (urban neighborhoods) and rural settlements in the era following the establishment of American rule, Tejanos combined tenets of Mexican tradition with those of American culture. The result was a Tejano community that practiced a familiar folklore, observed Catholic holy days and Mexican national holidays, spoke the Spanish language, yet sought participation in national life.

(From a May 4, 1998 article by Dr. Andrés Tijerina)

Benny Gordon, Tony & Dallas GOP Chairman Kenn George (Founder of RNHA Dallas)

PART II
DISSECTING MEX-TEX POLITICS

5

POLITICAL BIRTH IN TEXAS

Sen. John Cornyn & Tony

"According to the 1990 U.S. census, the number of Hispanics living in the United States totals more than 22 million. This figure includes an estimated four million undocumented aliens—immigrants who have entered the country illegally." By: Census Bureau

"Denial ain't just a river in Egypt."
Mark Twain 1835–1910

Illegal immigration seems to be a question that comes up often. Well, my answer is lets look at the whole picture, since the beginning of the time. People have been lured to this country because of the power that the United States possesses. That's right; we are the best, we are the brightest, and we are the strongest military power on the earth. If I lived in an impoverished country that offered few opportunities for my family, I would do everything to help earn a living for my kids. So the real questions is how do we get 12 million undocumented aliens to turn themselves in? Well the answer is "I don't know", because until we work with bordering countries to secure their borders we are wasting our time. A program that has been suggested that might work is a guest worker program, which allows illegal workers to apply for residency. Senator John Cornyn of Texas developed a program that could partner with certain industries to allow guest worker programs. Even in the Era of National Security it is still important that we maintain Economic Security. September 11th made us stronger as a nation, and with the strong leadership of our President, we can achieve everything we need. That is why I supported the Matricular Consular, here in Dallas. The Department of Treasury and the Transportation Security Administration supported it. So I too support this, I don't allow bias when it comes to protecting National security.

In the city of Dallas for example, I led the effort to help bring in the Identification card, and have it passed by the City Council. I remember that on October 7, 2003 a discussion was brought up about the identification card at a Public Safety Committee of the Dallas City Council and the members present were Dr. Elba Garcia, Chair, Gary Griffith, Vice-Chair, John P. Loza, Mayor Pro Tem, Donald W. Hill, Deputy Mayor Pro Tem, James L. Fantroy, Council member, Sandy Greyson, Council member, Mitchell Rasansky, council member. The discussion involved the safety of the card. I simply stated that as a citizen and proud leader of the Pachyderms, we needed to pass this piece of Resolution in order for the city to move forward with economic advances into all communities. This resolution would allow thousands of residents to pay fines, and continue with their lives in Dallas County. Programs like this would allow citizens to pay their bills without fear of retaliation or arrest. My biggest feeling is that until we as a nation can grow independently economically, financially we will be dependent on other nations to assist us with labor for those jobs in which there is a high demand. I currently support Guest worker programs and identification programs; I also feel they are long over due. Sometimes people think that guest programs are discriminatory; however I disagree. My family came during the "Bracero Program" and did well during the Eisenhower Administration. Here is a brief history, that's currently changing with all the activity going on in the world today.

During the 1960's, a family by the name of Delgadillo crossed the border on a second visit to restart work in the fields. Mission, Texas home of the Eagles, which Tom Landry was a coach, became the starting point of a journey, which would take everyone to the "North" as they would call it. Apples, Oranges, strawberries and sunflowers, were the order of the day. What people don't realize is that contracts were giving to families that moved and worked the fastest in the fields. So for twelve months the Delgadillo family would move from Washington State to California and eventually working their way back to Texas. Work and toil, was all that waited most families in the Valley. Politics was the last thing on their mind. Vietnam, and all the craziness that followed here in the United States did not even affect any, working the fields. Getting paid was the politics of the day. A group that introduced themselves to everyone were field aides who turned out to be agents for the Democratic Party. As everyone knows the Democrats controlled the Southwest and even what is known today as the Lower Rio Grande Valley-McAllen, Mission and Los Ebonos. Discrimination at the polls was common and fraud was common practice, the combination of these two things discouraged many Hispanics from registering to vote. Vote "Bosses" even required money to vote, and if you voted for their man, they'd cover the fee.

The tax was intended to keep the vote going one direction or another, Hispanics, many of whom were too poor to afford the tax often voted for the "bosses" choices. In areas with large Hispanic populations, voting district boundaries were often drawn to scatter the Hispanic voters over several districts. This practice, called gerrymandering, held down the percentage of Hispanic voters within any one district.

My mother tells of how during this era in the politically controlled state of Texas, the Democratic Party would muscle in the operatives to the border towns and force people to select their candidates or face losing the only job they could have. Citizen and Non-Citizen were bused in trucks and wagons to the nearest voting place and told to support the name that the patron had given them. It was done like this for years in the Lower Rio Grande Valley, cheating, lying and threats of violence.

During the 60's, four Mexican Americans won election to Congress and they were Senator Joseph Montoya of New Mexico and Representatives Eligio de la Garza, Henry B. Gonzalez of Texas and Edward R. Roybal of California.

Politics in Starr County didn't come through until the late 70's and even dragged into the late 90's with voter fraud. If you remember even in 2002,

Hidalgo County had the most deceased voter rolls then anywhere else in the country. It seems that the grand resurrection would occur on election date. If I remember, I believe my dead grandfather hasn't missed an election since he's gone to heaven almost 18 years ago. It is even rumored that a State Representative from Palmview places, a thank you card on his grave marker each election cycle. My late Aunt Anita mentioned this rumor to me. Who lived in Los Ebanos. This is no surprise considering the history of the Valley, should I mention Box 13, this box played a critical role in our nations history. Ever hear of President Lyndon B. Johnson. One tough mother, as I hear it. He could cuss and cut it cold just as fast. He did appoint several Hispanics to high government posts during the 1960's.

For example, Vicente T. Ximenes became chairman of the President's Cabinet Committee on Mexican-American Affairs. Johnson made Hector P. Garcia a member of the United States delegation to the United Nations and appointed Raul H. Castro United States ambassador to El Salvador.

When outreach efforts reach into various communities success can be seen by everyone—whether it was President Eisenhower or Nixon. One little kept secret in Dallas is the help that the Nixon Administration played in a barrio clinic in West Dallas. That's right President Richard Nixon the man that some Republicans won't even talk about. President Nixon was a good man in my view. Why you ask because I owe my vaccinations to a clinic called Los Barrios Unidos Clinic. Back in the 70's I received my immunizations and dental work, at Los Barrios Unidos Clinic. As a matter of fact when my whole family came to Dallas, we would walk through and get our shots and immunizations. Even today, thousands of children walk in and get their medical needs taken cared of by the clinic. Started by a quite president, Richard Nixon, say what you will but to this day there is not even a mention or plaque commemorating his help.

One little story that my sister Anna remembered was the time we met John Zapata Gonzales, a grassroots civil rights leader who fought to open the clinic. One day while sitting in the waiting room, a homeless man was bothering my sister Kathy, and Anna along with myself would tell this man to stop. I believed we three could have kicked his butt, but out of nowhere John appeared. My sister commented it was like superman, the man of steel, coming to the rescue. With a couple of combinations and left jabs' the mean man left.

John was a big man who learned the basics about civil rights in a boxing ring fighting in the Golden Gloves on Saturdays. I feel his brief stretch in the Marines prepared him to deal with the problems of any big city. He commented to me that you can work with everyone most of the time, it's the devil inside you need to watch out for. How true were his comments, in a big city like Dallas.

Today you can find him walking around east Dallas with a stick in his hand marching voters to the polls. During off election cycles he's pushing for improved schools in Dallas, and ensuring that kids stay the focus considering that more then fifty five percent of Hispanics drop out of school before graduating.

Some people don't realize that President Ronald Reagan helped to expand the horizon in education and advancement for Hispanics-even making history by offering the only General Amnesty to illegal immigrants in 1986. He expanded business opportunities and secondary education. It was Ronald Reagan that was known for kicking ass, and taking names. If you were honest and true, you'd have to admit that Reagan made America a force to reckon with. Peace through Strength.

President George Bush continued the tradition by expanding trade and relations with Mexico and other parts of South America.

Even the current President George W. has broadened the administration to include all those that have been given a call to keep. History is funny because it is changing daily, and for me to include everything we would never finish. Economics, education, and opportunity ensure success for all. Not just a few. Leaders that are suppose to stand up and ask questions simply sit and relax while others shoulder the burden.

6

DEFINITIONS &QUESTIONS

Anna, Att. Gen. Gregg Abbot & Katherine

"There are only two ways to live your life. One is as though nothing is a miracle. The other is as though everything is a miracle."
—Albert Einstein 1879–1955

A letter recently sent to me came from some students attending a political science class from the University in Mexico City. They had heard of the great artist running for political office. After telling them that I was not the actor or singer, I answered their questions. A question that came was what are Mexicos and how do they impact politics to come.

Well let's look at the question and definition if one exists. Mexicos, the word Mexicos may not appear to be important but we should all learn it because remember that 4 million individuals are showing up and we need to fully understand where they're coming from. There are four or five distinct societies in Mexico.

The gap between these societies is so wide that one suspects that it is equivalent to the dimensions of the caste system in developing countries in the Far East.

To the everyday individual one might guess that progressively the caste system of Mexico is recreated just south of the border. In towns such as Monterrey and Mexico City it is normal and not uncommon for class systems to be in place. I believe that in about 10 or 20 years a class system will be in effect throughout the Southwest. We might call this the "distant Mexico" effect, one brought about by my entering into one of the worlds of the distant neighbors of Mexico. What's happening in Mexico, as well as in any other country, is concerned with the preservation of national sovereignty and economic security.

In Mexico, national security policy strengthens national sovereignty and military security through the mechanism of making Mexico's political system invisible. Just as a dog bites an intruder, it can be very interesting when it comes to politics of the future.

Take for example the notion that when the United States or Canada look south they have the same idea, identity that mirrors itself. Such a policy works largely because Great Powers are vulnerable to deception on account of vanity.

To make Mexico invisible to American eyes—not for one year or for one presidency—but for generations to come, political institutions and standard conventions must be established and maintained. Together, these institutions and conventions must consistently pull off the magician's trick of making audiences believe that, with their own eyes, they have seen what never in fact existed. How is this trick accomplished?

The first means is through the use of American political vocabulary in Spanish that can be easily translated into English by recently arrived journalists, diplomats, and executives. This basket of terms, which is for export as well as domestic markets, which include the following examples: presidente, candidato, partido, elección, voto, estado, congreso, senador, constitución, suprema corte.

Long answer for such a short question, but one must remind themselves that systems of known government follow the individuals that once were governed.

In Mexico, members of the politically conscious classes speak, not Spanish, but a little-understood code language. The use of code language in Mexican politics is meant to keep Mexico invisible to the United States. Additionally, the use of code language helps keep the political classes in power: for the remaining 75% of the Mexican population the code language is as indecipherable as it is others from the States.

When Mexican and foreign political analysts comment that the so-called "electoral strength" of the PRI lies in the countryside where close elections are routinely won by the PRI, they fail to mention that the politically illiterate countryside has virtually no comprehension of Mexican national politics or institutions. That's right the politically illiterate, the simple individuals that have no care in the world. Remember the poor just want one thing, the opportunity to be heard and the idea that things will get better.

Visual Marketing and branding are very popular with the PRI party. Just like Coke is known worldwide or McDonalds can be seen in India. Branding is becoming popular, in Mexico.

Just like the phrase "Fresh Air", states its fresh and free but who decided that it was "Fresh". I laugh sometimes when questions regarding state politicians and area Judges comes to brand identification.

Republican and Democrat have become the new PRI and PAN of the Southwest. The PRI logo in the minds of the campesino is one of nationalism, patriotism, and liberal ideas, not one of making discriminating choices about candidates or party platforms. While the PAN logo represent the conservatives and religious right of the community.

When it comes to business and open borders PAN is the most open to change. PRI on the other hand represents the old guard. Consider a recent statement made by PRI officials to peasants in the State of Chiapas: "La pobacion de Chiapas en las areas rurales tiene uno de los mayores indices de rezago en materia del bienestar del hogar." Freely translated, the statement reads, "The rural population of Chiapas has one of the greatest indexes of backwardness in family income." The peasants must have heard something about "one of the greatest" but the rest of it was a mystery, as no one with a minimal formal education will have the slightest idea of what an index is; further, the term "rezago" is not one generally understood by the lower class majority of Mexico.

MexTex politics, is principally the struggle among competing localities power by persons who have mastered the Mexican Veda. In part it is about performing a perpetual magic show for U.S. audiences. Finally, it is about the actions of persons and organizations that are either semi-literate or entirely illiterate in the history, interpretation and hermeneutics of the text of the Mexican epic. Mexican society may be compared to the society of the Manchu dynasty (1644-1912): only a small percentage of the population (perhaps 5%) was literate, that is, was taught to read and write Chinese characters; women were not taught to read or write, and their feet were bound, much like their intellects; finally, the Mandarin class imposed a strict Confucian constitution.

In Mexican terms, this system of social organization succeeds in safeguarding Mexico's national security and assuring a reasonable freedom of maneuver of Mexico's Mandarin class. The politically uneducated masses of India, China and Mexico, meanwhile, remain sunk in their fatalism; holding to the view that events happen by individual or collective karma.

Political control in Mexico is the system of centralized information. The idea is that if there is only one supplier of economic and statistical information, the marketplace of consumers has to accept government-controlled prices and quality, where quality refers to accuracy and reliability.

Some people have questioned my ideas but it makes perfect sense when you realize that your next voting block is moving in from the South. If masses of Canadian's were coming in daily, then I'd be giving a history lesson on French Hierarchy and how to deal with upset citizens from Toronto. Speaking of Toronto, well I won't go there.

Deep Down as it's called refers to the United Mexican States, as Mexico is officially called, is a federal republic consisting of 31 states and the Federal District of Mexico City. Executive power is in the hands of the President, who is elected every six years by adult citizens, and the Cabinet he appoints.

The National Congress consists of a Chamber of Deputies and the Senate. The 500 deputies of the Chamber are elected for 3 year terms; the 128 Senators for a 6 year term. Each state has its own constitution, and is administered by a governor elected for 6 years and Chamber of Deputies.

Elections are, however, anything but free and fair. The power of local PRI officials in all aspects of economic activity ensures a certain degree of support from voters 'repaying debts'. Fraud is also widespread. Here are but a few examples of politics in the deep down south as they say. Way back in 1988, the government's presidential candidate looked set to lose to opposition candidate Cuauhtémoc Cárdenas (PRD) until the computers 'broke down' in the middle of the count.

Imagine your local candidates "taking out" each other over lunch. Political assassinations are frequent. Difficult opposition at home, such as the students in 1968, has been literally murdered. The use of violence as a political tool also occurs within the ruling elite, the murder of PRI presidential candidate Luis Donaldo Colosio in 1994 is generally attributed to others in the tension-ridden party.

Mexico's governing party pledges to turn over a new leaf every year by making its first presidential primary open, clean and fair. But since candidates of the past like Francisco Labastida Ochoa seem to be the past president's choice, many old guard party leaders backed him with the dirty electoral tricks that have kept the party in power for 70 years until Fox.

Party chiefs in one gulf coast town ordered a municipal bulldozer to block the road leading to a rally for Labastida's main rival, Roberto Madrazo Pintado. Some schoolteachers nearby were given time off to help in Labastida's campaign.

Elsewhere, a popular radio talk show host was forced off the air after broadcasting an interview with Madrazo. More recently television newscasts, strongly influenced by the government, gave Labastida overwhelmingly lopsided coverage. And all across Mexico, state governors and town mayors from the governing Institutional Revolutionary Party, known as the PRI, have been handing out groceries, building supplies and other gifts to buy votes for Labastida. Talk about cost cutting savings, you won't find at the local supermarket. Imagine one day waking up to the sounds of Wal-Mart's cost cutting and suddenly there was a 50% mark down if you went out and voted. I can guarantee that everyone in my neighborhood would be crashing down the street to get to the polls.

You have to remember that stories and tales down South are common, they even happen in towns like San Antonio or McAllen or even Houston. I remember personally that during the Orlando Sanchez mayoral race. The opposition was bussing and even paying for taxicabs for people to go vote.

So one does not need to travel far to get some old fashioned politics. If you remember way back during the last few elections. I was studying the international elections and reviewed a case that involved the late term of President Ernesto Zedillo, who all knows broke ranks and surprised everyone in the government when he renounced the lengthy tradition by which Mexican presidents, who are limited to one six-year term, handpicked their successors.

Surprisingly, you'll remember that the U.S. economy was shifting in the southwest and for two months there was debate on who would rule in the south.

Suddenly, my uncle called me and stated that PRI scheduled its first primary election for the first time in the countries history. And even more surprising was the perception that it was all a show for the business community. In Mexican political tradition, every six years after the president announced the new PRI candidate, a ritual followed: "la cargada," or the charge, in which party leaders rushed to publicly proclaim obsequious loyalty to the future president. Every 6th year it's the usual, like ordering a chicken fried steak, its tastes good but no surprises. This year, with party rules guaranteeing equal competition in the primary.

The winner of the PRI primary had a strong shot at becoming president of Mexico in the general elections. The party has used those tactics in several recent state elections. In the state of Mexico, which surrounds Mexico City, for instance, one in every three voters who cast ballots for governor in July said they had received groceries. Funny how food, played a great role in getting out the vote, could it be a growing trend throughout the Southwest?

Hum, only one could imagine, food has always been a key that opens the mind. Heck, politicians in South Texas barbeque so much fajita's and sausage; I sometimes forget were the border ends and begins. An area state senator once blocked traffic for miles, and miles and you'd be surprised at the various methods of getting cold refreshment delivered to a countywide function.

Maria Dominguez, who is a grass-roots organizer in Dallas who works on various campaigns, commented on the adventures she went through during one election. "They do lottery drawings, they hand out scholarships, roof tins, and groceries. And all these things come from our own back yard here in Dallas.

Dr. Mintu once told me that marketing is the key to a successful campaign regardless of the product. Food, Cars, Clothing, have a value given by the amount of promotion and marketing afforded the product. I revisited her at the Texas A&M University complex outside of Mesquite, and she was surprised. Last she heard, I was traveling through Houston on my way to Midland.

Sometimes when I'm sharing advice on Hispanic Politics, I pick up unusual items for her to take to class. So for this class I dedicate this chapter to her and all the students in her Marketing Program.

Coca-Cola gives us a perfect example of true marketing at its finest. Imagine the marketing might of a company that not only offers a solid soft drink worldwide but also even helps a president get elected. That's right, the big cowboy of the South turned out to be a former Coca-Cola executive. He has brought Mexican politics a new change.

Everywhere Fox traveled, he was greeted with the same shrieking enthusiasm, the same glowing faces and the same optimism. He is a master campaigner. One benefit of the 71-year reign of the Institutional Revolutionary Party (P.R.I.) is that it controls the levers of Mexico's political machine, which makes Fox something of an outside chance. But since he did beat out the PRI's candidate, the decidedly less macho Francisco Labastida Ochoa, Fox has certainly changed Mexican politics.

Dr. Mintu mentioned to me one time in class that the key to success is the brand identification and marketability. Image is key, change a known image, and the public is sure to notice. Coke for example should have been a key prime example for Fox to follow. When Coke went to "New Coke", the public revolted and sales fell allowing Pepsi to break in. Suddenly, Coca-Cola had to decide fast on the return path. Suddenly, they restarted Coke Classic. Image is one thing that is hard to recover from if it is tarnished over time. But product loyalty is quick to fade if change is unexpected. Fox who was driven by personality and powerful emotions and promises for educational revolution, better health care for the country's poor and a stable economy for its businessmen. Allowed some advisors to change his product mid-stream during his administration. How ironic or poetic is it to repeat in political history, let's fast forward and leap for a status report for today.

Fast-forward to modern day, October 11,2005, Fox is rebounding and PAN has lost more seats to political rivals. In my view he needs to remember that with Coke there was always Pepsi, with PAN there's always PRI. To get people to stay loyal, they have to believe in a service geared towards the people. I predict a slow upward return of PAN, but rivals will always duplicate and replicate ideas to suit their own agendas. In time people will eventually see the Real deal.

In conclusion, should we be concerned about Mex-Tex politics. Because the good ole' days of Huey from Louisiana seem to be spilling into the entire Southwest. We must educate the voter, and be very mindful of the struggle that some new visitors have gone through. Before we go and complain, why don't more Hispanics vote? Let's educate the voters on the future of not voting.

The Three Amigos

"The truth is more important than the facts."
—Frank Lloyd Wright 1868–1959

7

"OUTSIDE THE BOX"

Margerie Ford, Lt. Gov. David Dewhurst & Anna

"Half this game is ninety percent mental."
—Yogi Berra

In this chapter, we examine the concept of outside the box. I will showcase some examples that truly represent the strategy.

When most people think outside of the box, the results can be very interesting.

Look at the recent headlines that flooded the airwaves.

The California Recall, Arnold for Governor, the outcome "Victory for Arnold and Hasta La Vista for Davis". Will Arnold prepare for his next challenge and win a re-election bid to retain the state of California. Or will he think beyond to a senate race opportunity.

Even General Clark jumped into the race for the 2004 presidential race against ten or so opponents. He didn't win, but he tried and maybe again in 2008.

During my review I examined a question asked to me by e-mail concerning President Bush. The question was, "Outside thinking has helped the President, Why?"

Well to start, one must examine the values that Americans are craving: Strength, Power, and Confidence. Americans want strength and unity in the country, so outside thinking is it.

These core elements are generally exhibited by those that think outside the box. Do you remember sometime back in the mid 90's a Governor by the name of Jesse "The Body" Ventura?

He shocked Minnesota's political establishment by winning the gubernatorial election. I still remember that night, it was windy and even exciting, considering that I was standing outside of the newly elected state representative Betty Browns office in downtown Greenville, Texas.

During her run for state house I was President Emeritus of the College Republicans at TAMU-Commerce. Some of the club members were split on the support of the future governor, but I remember that night like no other.

We were sitting on the sidewalk, waiting for some of the poll numbers to come in. Mike Mote, John Fugitt, Jenny Reynolds, and my other friend Greg Hendrickson, were standing around after running around all day putting last minute fliers around town.

Suddenly our discussion went from being tired and exhausted to political reviews on the Minnesota's gubernatorial race.

Some of the views expressed revolved around his experience or his physical appearance.

I simply stated, "In today's world we need to be focused on energizing the country, and not allowing old ideas to bog us down into another depression."

Jesse the Body Ventura would serve as a great Governor and make his state great. So to State Rep. Betty Brown would win and even fight off a challenge in 2006. The same argument had been made with her campaign. Some in the Hunt County area even doubted her victory. Why? Because some in Kaufman County, felt she was a women.

So as President Emeritus of TAMU-Commerce, I had an international parade in the center of the campus and played drums and waved flags. I even publicly declared from that day forward that candidates belonging to the Republican Women of Texas would receive extra help in a run for office. It is in my view that women have struggled to be accepted in the workplace and even in the political arena. Back in College, one rule stood firm with me, if we're gonna date, then you better own a shotgun. Most Republican Women I've dated can out shoot just about any of my friends. So when I'm invited to a Ranch to hunt, be pre-pared, the girl holding the rifle is going to tell the whole town she kicked your butt during season.(As a side note, if your not a hunter, you won't understand. If you lose during a competition, you'll end up buying dinner for the whole family, and have to listen to them joke about you)

My club was so recognized for stepping forward and admitting that equality for women in the Republican Party needed to go beyond talk and move to action. Even the campus faculty was surprised at the turnout.

Secondly, the best surprise is when Sen. Phil Graham of Texas turned out for a reception praising the club and promoting Betty Brown.

Well out of the box thinking did win and will win 99% of the time.

Any issue regardless of nature must be examined through the eyes of many, but decided on by a few. That's right the key to development, is pooling ideas and coming up with a plan, and taking action.

Out of the box thinking is more of a strategy, which is applied to multiple issues. Take unconventional subjects or issues such as the Star Wars Missile Defense System or the Salt I Treaty or NATO. These issues were unique and beneficial to the United States.

Just imagine for instance if our military or economy was singular in nature, and trade was limited! The reality would be utter chaos, and economic stagna-tion.

Today's global society requires leaders such as the United States, to exercise action rather then reaction.

Whether it's politics, economics, defense or simply a project for the local church. You must stand alone, sometimes in order for society to withstand the burden of "Stale Ideas and the mass of Dead Horses".

Even today as I recall some of the discussions at the time were about politics and trade. NAFTA, (North Atlantic Free Trade Agreement) had even been passed and discussed as a possible alternative for doing business.

Trade between the United States and Mexico has almost doubled since 1994, when both countries and Canada signed the North American Free Trade agreement, or NAFTA.

Agreement's which at the time were outside of the box. Generally, individuals who work outside of the box are the innovators and the leaders.

Minnesota for example led the nation in electing an outsider and independent. Politicitosis is an illness that affects voters of all backgrounds into voting for the outsider. Not only has Politicitosis affected Minnesota during Ventura's reign as governor, but California's governor race also. It seems that a strand of the virus affected the mostly Democratictily held state into voting in Arnold for their leader.

The only problem is that when you elect someone who's outside the box, you end up with an individual rather then a system of individuals. For example, when Jesse the body planned his tour to Mexico, Ventura met with U.S. trade representative Charlene Barschefsky.

Some will recall in reports and stories of how even the new governor was asked to try and promote the trade policy in Washington D.C.

Well you can imagine the response that went across the news wires everywhere. His comments were quite interesting. And I'll quote from some of the reports sent via Internet and newspapers, which stated Ventura's statement as:

"I don't see myself really carrying the nation with me, I haven't been instructed to do so by any higher-ups. I'm here on behalf of the state of Minnesota, and will work for the state of Minnesota. Let the other 49 do their own work too."

Can you imagine that, an outsider telling the Federal government to hustle his or her plan to someone else. Leadership was exercised that day, because most individuals without principles would have caved in and shoved the people of Minnesota aside.

What style, and leadership, Ventura exercised. Even now while I'm drinking coffee at my desk, I just reviewed an old copy of USA Today story by Kathy Siely, which read "Schwarzenegger wins as Calif. Revolt ousts Davis", the only comment noted by Arnold that I read from him was "Sweep out the special interests and don't increase taxes."

Even Schwarzenegger set the tone in California.

Just imagine being married to a relative of the Kennedy Clan and winning the governors race knowing full well that your wife's uncle is campaigning against you.

How sweet the victory must be, overcoming obstacles and pressure from all around.

In conclusion, regardless of the struggle or mission that is set in motion. Outside thinking will always benefit those willing to take the risk and try. How sad it is for those that never leave the box of "fear". So if you wanted to paint, sing, or simply run for office. Just do it!!

Don't wait for society to agree on what's normal, because life is like a book. Would you buy a book that talked about your life?

I hope the answer is yes!

PART III
POLITICAL MUSINGS

Tony & George Dawson

8

"W" & THE FUTURE

"It's not the size of the dog in the fight,
it's the size of the fight in the dog."
—Mark Twain 1835–1910

Is "W" the future? Is George W. Bush the Answer? Does he have a mission on uniting the country?

The answer is Yes! Yes! And his mission on uniting the country is to reach to the unreachable go places that are unthinkable. Will the critics agree, probably not, even today while watching FOX news polls show the Presidents poll as taken hits on his popularity on Iraq.

But, regardless I still feel that the mission in Iraq was needed. It's my view.

For years Hispanics have been perceived as natural one party believer, and that the Democrats have held the minds for generations to come. There rs an old bumper sticker that I've seen around town that reads "When I learned to spell, I wrote my name. When I got a job, I became Republican".

That's right some may not find this comment funny, but I laughed for almost an hour. Let's examine my thoughts on George W. Bush, and since I'm the Hispanic audience and represent a pretty good idea of where America is going! When I watch the President speak,

President Bush balance's challenges with opportunities that face everyone in this growing nation.

Sometimes, W' will discuss the importance of including all, which "all" represents the children that have been left behind in the educational roller coaster.

The roller coaster for some could be a failing system or a lifestyle that has dealt constant struggles to overcome.

For example Bush's Literacy Program focuses on the early learner, and has dealt with this issue, which affects everyone. We have to remember that a community that allows its children to suffer has only itself to blame. The future is revealed clearly in the President's book, *A Charge to Keep*", and outlines his strategies on outreach.

I've read his book several times and have come up with my own theory on Bush Tactics.

For example, lets look at "W", during his run in Texas. Back then he lauded business leaders for creating hope for all.

Several years ago, a combination of his appeal and inertia conspired to help Bush win an unprecedented percentage of Latino votes in Texas. His success in Texas serves as a cautionary tale for Democrats across the country.

The GOP first began to emerge as a major force, in Texas politics during the first part of the Clements administration.

Dallas County was swept like a new storm in April, and left turn over for years. For example Judges like newcomers Tom Fuller and Bruce Woody came with over a landslide to become solid Judges over the years. Democrats locally thought that they could rely indefinitely on the traditional loyalty of the state's growing Mexican-American population.

Since the 80s, conventional wisdom has held that in order to win statewide elections, Democrats would have to offset the Republican urban vote by garnering large margins of victory in heavily Latino south Texas. But that did not happen, even during 80's and early 90's the vote was swinging to the Republican majority.

Bush received 40 percent of the state's Latino vote, unprecedented for any Republican statewide. Texas Latinos in 1998 loved his message of compassionate conservatism. While much of Bush's appeal came by charming attitude about life and the devotion to common sense values and the belief in humanity.

I can remember the day Bush decided to run for governor, it was as if the "Bell tolled to the' and the Democrats felt doom.

Simply put Bush's opponents have always been psyched out, similar to how rival boxers can when before they get in the ring. Hispanic voters want meat in their message. Action, not words, and the last thing Hispanics want to see, is Weakness; in a President. It's almost a death sentence for a politician to show weakness.

Bush's one-time success in winning 40 percent of the Hispanic vote is specific to the governor and does not presage a Latino political mutiny toward the GOP.

However, it does provide an important model of how a strong, ethnically sensitive GOP candidate can capture significant numbers of Hispanic votes.

During my run for the State House in the same year that President Bush was running for office allowed me to make inroads into the Hispanic and African American Communities.

I can remember that as a Strong Hispanic Conservative Republican Candidate it would be difficult to reach out, if the message was not the same. I did the unusual and unthinkable.

I attended debates sponsored by the Unions and UAW and the NAACP. If there was a church that was in need of some positive words, I attended. My one promise was that if I were invited, I'd go and represent the party and myself. By utilizing the "Out of the Box" mentality, I was able to mobilize Southeast Dallas County into a voting bloc that to this day can swing county wide elections. Unfortunately, the Democratic party wasn't going to allow me to upset the apple cart. Millions of dollars was poured into Southeast Dallas, to undo the damage that I'd inflicted. But just as the sun shines, the light will always get through.

My opponent at the time was Dale Tillery. He was the big bad dog in the yard in District 105. Well I guess he met the second biggest dog in the neighborhood. He must of spent thousands of dollars to defeat me.

All I did was yard signs, and a few highway signs and basic little stuff. My opponent was also flanked by a big State Senate race, and a huge Congressional race that pitted Congressmen Pete Sessions against Regina Montoya-Coggins, and Dr. Bod Duell against State Senator David Cain. It was one of the worst election fights in my districts history. Signs were stolen and destroyed, even area Republicans were getting into fights with local democrats in front of the polling booths. My family was followed and chased down the highway by some energetic voters.

During all this excitement, I carried one simple message and that message was "Are you tired of taking it all the time, don't blame me blame yourselves".

Suddenly, long time 30-year democrats and locals got excited and attacked Dale Tillery's office with demands for change. Area cafes and barbershops carried my signs in the windows, and I was called the "Huey Long of Southeast Dallas" that's right, the people had enough. What I didn't realize was that my advertising had spread from my little district to about the entire North Texas Area. People as Far East as Texarkana would e-mail me asking where to go vote. Some people thought that I was running for the U.S. Congress, and I simply replied no but maybe in the future. Right now my friend Pete Sessions needs your vote.

I visited with the President when he came to town for a visit, at Southern Methodist University. His speech was excellent and stated one principle, "A charge to keep, he commented that those individuals that have the opportunity to lead and exercise free will by taking action, rather then in-action will help America retain it's leadership as a superpower in the world.

So I carried that message back to my district, knowing that victory, was greater then myself. America and Texas would win by educating and stepping outside of the box to reach out to voters.

The question that is asked a lot is do I feel that President Bush has done a great job as President. My answer is still yes, are their improvements needed and my answer is yes.

Iraq still needs protection, and our trade policies need to include all of Americas. But I'm sure that he is thinking ahead. One day, I'd like to sit at his ranch in Crawford and eat some chili and play a game of chess.

Just like chess, Bush during his campaign is an excellent study, and would prove a great challenger. He's excellent at "Out of the Box" moves.

For example, Bush would change flights and strategy, and further implement the BushISTO move, when he visited places like El Paso, Del Rio and McAllen. Areas that were strong Democratic hot beds which most statewide Republican candidates routinely write off and which Democratic candidates long have taken for granted. Think of Bush as the "TORA, TORA" of politics.

There he tapped into the city's strong sense of isolation from Austin and made compelling arguments about how the future of Texas rests on the well being of the border region.

"Gov. Bush has given El Paso and the border unprecedented attention," says Mike Acosta, associate director of the Texas Centers for Border Economic Development. Rejecting the old images of the border as a haven for crime, drugs and pollution, Bush has argued that the region was an asset rather than a liability.

Because in Texas parlance the border is synonymous with Mexican Americans, this economic message has ethnic implications.

"When you say the border is good, you're saying Mexicans are good," says Thomas Longoria, a political science professor at the University of Texas at El Paso. "When you say the border is worth investing in, you're saying that Mexicans are worth investing in."

Nevertheless, many voters felt that Bush's mere attention to the region was enough of a reason to vote for him.

During his election in November, the governor received 39 percent of the Mexican-American vote in El Paso, enough to put him over the top and make him the first Republican gubernatorial candidate ever to win there. Carlos Ramirez, the Democratic mayor of El Paso, who endorsed the governor's reelection campaign, claims that Bush's Hispanic outreach has made the Mexican-American vote more competitive than before. "You can't vote straight ticket anymore," he says. "You have to exercise your political muscle." Bush still continues the strategy that he uses in his national campaign. Bush continues not only to court black and Latino business groups, but he regularly visits low-income schools and minority neighborhoods.

His speeches at these schools vary a lot from his standard stump speech, and still have more to do with substance.

How else to explain the campaign's recent unveiling of Spanish-language radio ads in Iowa? An unintended byproduct of Bush's "Tejano" strategy has been to give the Hispanic electorate more clout.

The same can be said for Latinos nationwide. The Bush campaign has forced traditional Democrats to scramble to get a front line defense to challenge him on.

The strategy is paying off, and as a general once commented that when pursued by your enemies from behind and surrounded by your enemies in front. The only strategy is to wait for early dawn and simply stampede your way through the middle of your opponent's camp and surprise them with sheer guts. It is only through surprise that the enemy will forget that they are soldiers and become human for a short time. Allowing your small army to run by.

9

WEAK IDEAS NEVER SUCCEED

John Zapata Gonzales and Tony Aguilar

"Never mistake motion for action."
—Ernest Hemingway 1899–1961

Had former Assembly Speaker Antonio Villaraigosa won his bid for mayor of Los Angeles last June, he would have become the highest profile Mexican-American politician in the country. He would have also become a symbol of the emergent left-labor-Latino alliance that some argue represents the future of politics in heavily Mexican-American regions of the country. "Villaraigosa's campaign embodies not just the hopes for a rising Los Angeles progressive politics," wrote Marc Cooper in The Nation. "It has taken on national significance as well." Harold Meyerson echoed these sentiments in The American Prospect. Yet as close as Villaraigosa came to capturing City Hall—he placed first in April's primary election—the notion that Mexican-Americans would lead a liberal revolution in West Coast politics was never more than wishful thinking.

While no ethnic or ideological movement swept the city last July, Los Angeles did move quietly—and quite naturally—into a new political era as City Attorney Rocky Delgadillo became the first Latino to assume citywide office in more than a century, Alex Padilla was elected city council president, and Councilman Nick Pacheco was selected to chair the city's powerful Budget and Finance Committee. Contrary to breathless news analyses of the election, it is really these New Democrats who represent the future of Latino politics in the West.

In June, *Newsweek* glibly called James K. Hahn's June victory over former Speaker of the California Assembly Antonio Villaraigosa in the mayoral race a "brownout." Disappointed partisans implied that L.A.'s "Latino future" had somehow been dimmed.

Yet equating Villaraigosa's candidacy with the culmination of a massive demographic shift not only unduly burdened Villaraigosa's candidacy, it mistook the part for the whole. It also reduced the region's ongoing ethnic transition to a zero-sum game in which, presumably, there are winners and losers.

Leading the media drumbeat about the region's ethno-political metamorphosis, the *Los Angeles Times* fundamentally misunderstood the evolutionary nature of cultural and ethnic fusion. Perhaps in a search for drama, its reporters wrote of the city as if it were neatly divided between the old and new and on the verge of some cataclysmic break between the two.

While Villaraigosa himself sought to position himself as a post-or pan-ethnic candidate, the media rarely mentioned his name without placing the adjective "Latino" before it. Thus, in the public imagination, the former union activist and local ACLU chapter president who received the backing of groups like the National Organization of Women and the Sierra Club became an all-encompassing symbol for Mexican-American political aspirations.

And, indeed, the possibility of electing the first Mexican-American mayor since 1872 excited Latino voters throughout the city. While Villaraigosa forged an impressively diverse list of endorsements, which included billionaires Eli Broad and Ron Burkle, as well as outgoing Republican Mayor Richard Riordan, the core of his support came from the city's left-labor-Latino alliance.

Over the last decade, labor unions have been instrumental in the political emergence of Latino Los Angeles. The Los Angeles County Federation of Labor, an umbrella organization representing some 800,000 workers, emerged as perhaps the most powerful force in Southern California politics. Putting an army of committed volunteers to work in campaigns for Congress, the state legislature, and the city council helped garner an impressive string of victories for both Latino and non-Latino pro-labor candidates.

But the growing share of Latinos in the union ranks as well as the emergence of high-profile Mexican-American labor officials has created the misleading impression that Mexican immigrants have high rates of unionization. In fact, foreign-born Latino males are the least likely to be organized of any group of men in Los Angeles County, while Anglo males are the most likely. Still, in many immigrant communities, where residents are highly transient and civic associations—like homeowners groups or chambers of commerce—are relatively weak, unions can wield disproportionate influence in getting out the vote.

So, while Villaraigosa's most enthusiastic constituency was made up of Latino labor activists who helped prod voters to the polls, most of Villaraigosa's Latino support was based on ethnic and not ideological loyalty.

A week before the June run-off election, a Los Angeles Times poll indicated that 50 percent of Latino voters considered Villaraigosa more liberal than they were. Still, he received 82 percent of votes cast by Latinos. But Rocky Delgadillo, the pro-business, moderate Democrat running for city attorney (the city's second highest elected post), pulled in nearly as many, winning 79 percent of Latinos and showing that Latino voters were more interested in asserting their ethnicity than a single ideological bent.

But even if Los Angeles' labor-left-Latino alliance had catapulted Villaraigosa into City Hall, it still would have represented the last hurrah of a generation-old activist dream rather than the future for Latinos in American politics. While the former Assembly speaker's ecumenical style did represent a breakthrough in Latino politics, his campaign's strategy has never proven successful for Mexican-American candidates.

Tony & Dr. Elba Garcia

10

TONY TACTICS 101

Luis De La Garza   Lt. Gov. David Dewhurst   John Gonzales   Tony Aguilar

**North Texas Republican
Latino Advisory Council**

"Now it is required that those who have been given a trust must prove faithful."
1 Corinthians 4:2

HISTORY IS IMPORTANT, BECAUSE it tells of one's mission in life. I felt that after my campaign run for the Texas House of Representatives, I'd give my secrets away so that other generations may use them in their run for office. Secondly, as the quote clearly states it truly is important for those with experience share with those that have a desire to reach out and help others.

During my travels some of my friends asked me to include some basic simple steps on how to outreach to the Hispanic community. So I included some history, strategy, ideas and forecast and then some closing recipes. Together they form the working battle plan for steps to outreach in any campaign.

Judge Woody, Luis Lara, Tony, Kenn George & Charles Lingerfelt

Quotes from the
"Art of war"

Invincibility lies in the defense; the possibility of victory in the Attack.
One who sets the entire army in motion to chase an advantage will not attain it.
There has never been a protracted war from which a country has benefited.
He who knows when he can fight and when he cannot, will be victorious.
If ignorant both of your enemy and yourself, you are certain to be in peril.
One defends when his strength is inadequate; he attacks when it is abundant.
Do not press an enemy at bay.
Know your enemy and know yourself and you can fight a hundred battles
without disaster.

TONY 101

1. Create Outreach Committee.

Tony feels your committee should be a team of local leaders who would be willing to volunteer time toward this effort. Invite the committee to review grassroots efforts that will take place within the membership. Make sure that each committee member understands that he or she is part of a local movement to raise the awareness of a local candidate or issue.

1. Local Analysis.

Tony feels the campaign is designed to be adapted at the local level. The key to adopting messages and strategies is creating a local situation analysis that will be used as a touchtone for creating your local action plan. It is important that you thoroughly assess the local situation, determining the strengths and weaknesses of the existing activities that your state, regional or city associations or divisions may be undertaking. By asking the committee to discuss the questions on the situation analysis, you will begin to develop a framework to help your committee allocate resources.

1. Assign Campaign Responsibilities.

Tony feels that each member of the campaign committee is assigned a specific task. Generally, they fall into the following categories:

Advertising Chair

Tony feels the campaign provides opportunities for paid print, radio and television placement at the local level. The advertising chair is responsible for raising funds from fellow supporters and others to place such ads. The advertising chair should solicit an advertising subcommittee to assist in these efforts. It is not necessary for these individuals to serve on the campaign committee, which is charged with total campaign oversight, but will only assist in raising funds for the advertising portion of the campaign. The advertising chair can meet separately with the subcommittee, establish goals and report progress to the campaign committee. This allows the committee to begin involving others in the campaign.

Issues/Media Relations

Tony feels that free media coverage for the campaign is just as important as paid media. The issues/media chair will identify media opportunities and serve as the primary local media liaison. The issues/media chair will be the primary campaign spokesperson for media comments and questions and will be asked to help identify opportunities for appearances on radio and television public affairs programs, letters to the editor, and Op/Eds, to name a few. It is not necessary for the media chair to participate in all of the interviews. It is more important to schedule the most informed and engaging representatives for the campaign who can communicate the messages most effectively.

Community Chair

Tony feels it is critical that the campaign committee network with groups such as local chambers of commerce, Rotary, and women's organizations, among others. The community outreach chair should develop outreach opportunities and presentations for these groups regarding the value of getting out the vote. The community outreach chair will coordinate contacting appointed and elected officials and other opinion-leaders who play a role. When elections are held, the outreach chair will help organize forums and discussions with candidates to help educate those who will eventually represent the community.

Build Contact List

Tony feels that a database that includes mailing addresses, fax numbers, phone numbers and e-mail addresses and membership in key organizations or offers of assistance to the campaign.

The e-mail is the best when communications are necessary if an immediate response is warranted. If you have newspaper or magazine articles or other reading material you want to share with your key contacts, you will want to mail packets to each.

It is important that you have all of the possible communication tools in a notebook or database for quick response and easy retrieval.

Developing the key contact list:

- Elected officials

- Civic Leaders

- CIVIC organizations

- Business leaders

- Local Media

Tony says once you have compiled the key contacts in each of these areas; prioritize them keeping in mind the number of potential contacts that the campaign committee can manage. Be sure to select messages and materials for each key contact with care.

Create Action Plan.

Tony feels that you'll need an action plan for each priority target. Some will require personal meetings while others will need presentations by multiple members of the committee. It may be necessary to conduct a seminar for some key groups, or write letters to the editor to communicate the message.

In organizing the campaign committee, begin to assign committee members to participate in the various methods of contact. If the committee is large enough, you might create teams to work together on presentations, workshops and letter campaigns. Even if forming a campaign committee is not a viable option in your community, it is still important to work through the process of analyzing your local situation and determining who and how to go about contacting key target audiences.

Fundraising for Activists

All campaigns and projects need some materials and resources to keep them running and to expand. It is a really good idea to consider fund-raising a part of your campaign right from the start and to make it enjoyable.

Fund-raising plan

First of all you need to work out how much money you need and by when. This will give you your fund-raising deadline. A good way to do this is to get everyone together and do a brainstorm on things the group needs. A brainstorm is a way of quickly gathering a large number of ideas. Start by stating the issue. Ask people to say whatever comes into their heads as fast as possible—without censoring it. Write these ideas on a large piece of paper and discuss them. Which things are most important to get? When do you need them by? Once you've got the list of things you need, do a second brainstorm on how to raise the cash/get the materials. Discuss these ideas and see which are most likely to work. Are there any ways in which you can get services/materials for free or cheaper? Do you have the necessary skills and the people to carry them out? The types of fund-raising you do will largely depend on the skills of the people involved. For example you might not find anyone to write a funding application, but you may know some artists who are willing to organize an auction of their artwork in support of your campaign. Fund-raisers not only help to raise resources but are also a great way of publicizing your campaign and getting new people involved. If you are putting on any events make sure people know what it is about and how they can get involved in the campaign or project.

Bank accounts

Depending on the type of fundraising it can be very helpful to have a bank account in the name of your group/campaign/project. People writing out checks feel a lot more comfortable if the money doesn't go into an individual's bank account. You will almost certainly need an account if you are applying to a founder for larger sums of money.

The account doesn't need to cost anything—building societies' savings accounts (pass books) are often a good choice. To open an association or society account you will need to show the building society/bank a constitution and an excerpt of minutes of a meeting enabling you to open one. You can get a standard constitution from the local group. You will need to insert your own objectives.

Some Fundraising Ideas

Getting things for free/cheap Before buying anything think about ways of getting it for free. Can you get stuff donated, on loan or through sponsorship? Here are some ideas:

Skips Are a great source for things like wood, plastic sheets, carpets and even furniture. Once you start looking, the amount of perfectly good stuff thrown out, particularly in wealthy areas, is overwhelming. If you spot something you want outside someone's house, knock on their door and ask. They often come up with even more stuff they want to get rid off. Similarly ask anyone working on a demolition site, or at the end of the day at a market if it's OK to take stuff from his or her skip. They'll probably say yes as it's cheaper for them than emptying it.

Wish List

A wish list is a list of all your needs with a plea for donations. It is a very easy way for people to help that cannot be there. Circulate the wish list as widely as possible. It is amazing how much useful stuff is lurking in people's attics and garden sheds—paint, wood, tools, cookers, stationary etc. Put everything down, including the boring stuff like socks and photocopier paper. Also ask for skills such as artists and welders.

Send it to any mail enquiries you get, distribute it to your mailing lists and put it on your stalls.

Discounts

Businesses may offer discounts to regular customers or people whose actions they support. Bulk orders of goods like whole foods, building materials, trees will be cheaper. Army surplus and junkyards are a good source of cheap clothes, boots, sleeping bags, tools, tarpaulins and other equipment. Remember In-Kind!!

Fundraising Events

Fundraising events can be a lot of fun for everyone involved. They include benefit gigs, jumble sales and garden parties. If well planned and attended, these events can raise lots of money and publicity for your group. Sometimes, however, they are a lot of effort and at the end of the event you will only have covered your costs, or even lost money! Here are some points to help you avoid that:

Publicity is the key to any good event: fly-post extensively, hand out flyers at other events, and try to get into the events listings of local media. Be creative and try to put a campaign spin on your fundraising. Remember that any organization or political candidate that can't maintain a list of at least 4000 e-mails plus. Will fall behind in the race to publicize. Boycotts such as the Dixie Chicks work well if the e-mail bank is working well. Individuals in California to New York can be advised in a matter of seconds rather then days. Also think about the timing of the event. Are any other local events happening at the same time? What about school holidays, bank holiday weekends and big sporting events such as the World Cup?

Make sure that people realize the objective of the event is to raise money so they don't try to freeload their way in! Think carefully about the admission fee. It must be enough to make money for the campaign, but not too expensive. Consider having a concessionary rate.

Fundraising events are a good way of getting new people involved, so make sure that you have an information stall at the event, with leaflets and displays, campaign merchandise and a collection tin for donations. You can also have these stalls at events by other people. If any sympathetic band is due to play in your area, or there is a regular club night at a local venue, approach them and ask if you can run a stall. Ask the band or DJ to point out your stall.

Benefit gigs—Most benefit gigs involve local bands or DJs. You will probably have to pay for the venue and a PA system. Find a band that is happy to be paid expenses only or you won't make a profit. Make sure that people realize the objective of the event is to raise money and don't try and brag their way in!

Sponsored events—An old favorite and good for publicity, but can take a lot of organizing. You could have a sponsored sports event, litter pick in a local park. Think up more creative ones and they will attract more people and money.

Raffles are easy to organize—you can make them part of any fundraising event you are organizing. First of all you'll need to source some prizes. They don't need to cost a lot and you can often get them donated. Find a friendly local business to give you a food hamper or two, gift tokens or free tickets to a local event. Ask some artists or crafts people to donate prizes. Or bake some delicious cakes.
You will also need raffle tickets. You can buy books of raffle tickets at many post offices and stationers. Then sell them for a pound or two at your event and a little later draw the prizes.

Sales—Consider having a stall at a fair or local fete, a car boot sale, plant sale, jumble sale or theme market. Get together well in advance to collect items to sell. Promote the stall as much as possible. On the sale make the stall look as attractive and welcoming as you can. Think about putting up a banner, so people know that they are supporting your campaign.

Campaign Merchandise T-shirts, badges, posters and postcards spread the message as well as raising money.

Appeals through your mailing list—In every newsletter or leaflet, mention the fact that your campaign needs money. Some people assume that if you are producing a newsletter then you must be doing all right. The truth is that campaign funding usually comes out of personal pockets. Always give clear instructions on how to donate, i.e. who to make checks and Postal Orders out to. Be aware that if you overdo it people may doubt your need. If the situation is really bad, you could put in a special leaflet stating your financial situation and ways that people could help. You could also put specific urgent appeals for money or goods on your info line.

Giving examples can help people identify with your situation and illustrate how every little helps. Always write personal thank-you letters to people who have sent money. Keep a record of all donors on your database. If you do a fundraising mail out to these people, remember to thank them for they're past generosity and give examples of what their donations have achieved.

Bucket rattling—At every event make sure you do some bucket rattling. Small change soon adds up and there are always people who will chuck in notes! Don't overdo it, or do it aggressively. Keep hold of your bucket. Don't do it at other people's events without asking first.

Benefactors—You may be fortunate enough to have a "benefactor" approach your campaign. People like this are rare and often prefer to remain anonymous. They may ask for a funding proposal or they may give freely.

Writing Funding Applications

Applying for a grant is often the only way to get larger sums of money. You could ask for funding for newsletters, organizational costs for event or action, office and staff expenses, action and communications equipment. Funding proposals for outrageous things are always worth a go—a hot air balloon or the use of a helicopter perhaps…

Which Founder?

There are many different organizations that give grants to small campaigns and projects. Your first step is to make a shortlist of those that are most likely to support your project or campaign. Nearly all founders have guidelines for giving out their money. These cover the kind of groups and activities they will fund, how much they will give and how to apply. There are a number of directories that provide information about founders. Your best bet however is to talk to other groups similar to your own to find out where they got their funding from.

Gathering Information

Once you've got your shortlist, find out as much as you can about these funders. What kind of activities do they fund, what are their criteria for giving out money, deadlines, forms, how much do they give. Is this the right founder to approach? They vary greatly in the stuff they require and how much money they give. If they've got a website or printed publicity materials, read them very carefully. Talk to people who have been able to get money from that founder but also to those that were turned down. Find out what works and avoid other people's mistakes.

Some funders only allocate funds once or twice each year, so find out when the next deadline is and how long it takes for them to decide. If you are looking for money to print leaflets next month then a founder who takes six months to make a decision is no good. If there are deadlines then make sure you keep to them!

When you're writing

Never write Dear Madam/Sir. Always find a name and check the spelling.

Project title—think of a snappy name for your project.

Grab their attention—and keep it! Funders are going to see hundreds of requests—make sure you stand out. Places to grab them are the cover letter and the summary.

Use the funder's language—be sure to use the same key words as they do. Confusion often results from using different words for the same ideas.

Be positive—never use "would", "could", "should", "might", or "may". Always use "will". If you don't have confidence in yourself and your project, they won't either.

Clear and easy to read. Organize the text in a clear structure so that everything flows smoothly. Avoid technical jargon and be concise. Do not rely on a computer spell-checker.

Be realistic—do not try to do too much. Show the proposal, for a "reality check".

Everything should be in **bite-size pieces**, small enough to swallow in one bite, but big enough for the reader to have to think about it. Use this especially in your expected results section.

<u>Comprehensiveness</u>—Make sure you provide all the information required. If you do not understand a question phone up and ask the funder.

<u>Relevance</u>—prove why the project is important in general and how it fits in with the funder's policies.

<u>Never send form letters</u> or general funding requests to funders.

<u>Make contact</u> with the funders—let them know, don't be afraid to ask questions. But think about what you are going to say beforehand Appear professional and remember to be nice to them.
letter to the funders. Building good relations will help you get more funding.

Cover Letter

This is your best chance to catch the attention of the founder, so make it concise, snappy and exciting. The cover letter is the first document the funder will read and it is often the basis for either consideration or rejection. The cover letter should state the name of the project, the goals of the project and the project in this case is getting elected or implementing a grassroots project. Don't forget to include your organization's name and address. A well-designed letterhead helps as well.

Project Summary

Sometimes called project description, this part is optimally only one page, and never more than two. It is a concise, hard-hitting, informative page which describes in brief who, what, where, why, when, how and the expected results. It should contain the following elements:

<u>Needs statement:</u> an overview of the needs (problems) your organization wants to address with the project/campaign. Describe briefly the overall context—this will help the reader to get a more complete picture of the scope of the problem. Use relevant facts, examples from the community or statistics to underpin your statement, but make sure all the data is correct. Identify who will benefit from you tackling these needs.

Goals and objectives: this section outlines what you will do to address the identified needs. This is where you set out your goals and objectives for the project. The objectives should be specific, tangible and measurable results.

Methods and timetable: How and when are you going to achieve the objectives of the project? Be very clear and realistic.

Why they should fund you: how does your proposal fit in with their funding policy? Have they supported you before? You may need to emphasize different aspects of your work for different funders, for instance some might be interested in you because you fall within their geographical area, others because the project falls within their sphere of interest.

Budget

It's possible to be too detailed and too vague with budgets. Each founder has different expectations so do ask. The budget consists of two parts: Costs and Income.

Costs: Main sections could include: staff and consultants' fees/salaries, publishing, equipment, running cost such as rent, telephone, heating, electricity and office supplies, insurance, travel, training. Don't forget the little things such as repairs on a photocopier every four months, etc. You may wish to just keep these topics without any more detail, but be sure to work everything out on another more detailed budget so that you can answer questions that may come up. Don't be afraid to ask for too much. If a founder likes a project but thinks it is too expensive they will quite often give you a percentage of what you asked for, or tell you to revise your figures. An application won't be rejected because of the budget, it will however be rejected if it is viewed as a bad investment. Do remember that you will have to keep receipts for all your spending—many funders want copies of these at the end of a project.

Income: List all the different bits of income that you expect. Some funders fund all the costs of the project, but many expect to you find up to 50% of the money from elsewhere. This could for example come from another founder, donations or membership fees. Luckily most funders accept contributions in kind—that is stuff/time people donate to the project. So if someone lends you a van for free, you estimate how much it would have cost you to hire it and put it down as contribution in kind. Get someone else to check it over. Also the total of the costs and the total of the income have to be the same figure.

Appended Information

Append any evidence such as: a time line and detailed work plans, your latest annual report, facts and figures supporting your case, letters of support from other organizations, an organizational chart, photographs and press cuttings. Choose these materials with care, make sure they support your application rather than undermine it!

11

TONY TACTICS PART II

**"Victory goes to the player who makes
the next-to-last mistake."**
—Chess master Savielly Grigorievitch Tartakower 1887–1956

Tony Strategy will help you to: Choose the right tactics at the right time.

Our first impulse is to throw ourselves into action straightaway. But if we take a little time to analyze the situation and to develop a plan of action we can increase our effectiveness and our chances of success. A strategy not only helps us to move from ideas to action but also to make the best use of people's time and energy. It will also help to prevent burnout and stop you from getting disillusioned half way through. A long-term plan means you can chart your successes—large and small—and appreciate them for what they are.

All actions have a positive and a negative impact—getting the balance right can be crucial. By looking at the medium and long term you can see which tactics will be useful and at what stage in the campaign/project they can be used.

Evaluate successes (or failures).

If you have a clear action plan you'll notice the milestones as you pass them. This is important for group morale, and helps to plan your future strategy.

Be consistent.

Your project should be seen to grow, rather than stop and start. This is important for group morale and to attract new people.

Evaluate offers of help/alliances/networks etc.

Is this the right time to accept concessions from your opponent? Is it worth compromising your position in order to work with other groups?

Match skills and energy to the tasks at hand.

By looking at skills and interests first you can come up with more exciting (and interesting) ideas for action than thinking of tasks and then delegating them. Once you have drawn up a strategy do be prepared to change it if necessary. Situations can change rapidly and require flexibility. It's also important to remember that the initial motivation is a good source of energy, and shouldn't be allowed get lost in endless discussions about what to do. A strategy is there to help you into action and not to immobilize you by causing long discussions.

Defining Your Aims

The first step on the road to strategy is to define your aims. What is it that you want to achieve? Your group's aim should be realistic and achievable. Spend some time in a relaxed atmosphere exploring people's personal motivations and developing the group's aim. Be aware that people's aims may be different from each other. Don't worry too much if your group can't come up with a united long-term vision, but you do need to agree on a common immediate or short-term goal to be able to work together.

Gathering more information

The next step is to gather more information. What do you need to know to achieve your aims? This could include environmental data, details about similar projects/campaigns or background information about companies/institutions/ people involved. Accurate information will not only help you make a good plan and give you ideas for action, but also help you to convince local people and potential allies. But don't get paralyzed by a mountain of irrelevant information…!

Identify Targets

In this part you are analyzing the information you have already gathered. Start by looking at all the different people and institutions that have an interest in the issue. Who are the people you need to talk to/convince/pressure to achieve your aim? Here is a very useful tool for this sort of analysis:

Tony Analysis

First, write the problem across the top of a big piece of paper. Draw a line along the bottom. This line is the *commitment line* and shows how strongly a party feels for or against the development. The left side of the paper is 'us' = strongly opposed, the far right is strongly in favor. People close to the middle are neutral towards the development.

Second, draw another line down the center of the page, top to bottom. This is the *power line* and shows how much influence a party has over the decision. The more power someone has the closer to the bottom they are.

Now plot the position of all the affected people, groups, institutions and authorities on the paper. What do you think is the position of local people, small shopkeepers, local newspapers, your group, and the developers? People may have power because of the law (like the council), or because of money (like the development firm), or because of commitment and beliefs (like us).

Think about the knock-on effects that would have.

In this example, local residents support your group, but aren't exercising much power. You have to think of ways of mobilizing the general public to bring them closer to the line. Doing this will also help to bring the local council further over to your side of the paper, since local people will begin to lobby the council—so by dragging the Local Residents dot down, you can also drag the Local Council dot a little towards you too. On the other hand, it will be very difficult to drag the Landowner, Development Company and local construction companies to the other side of the neutral line. What you can do, however, is push them away from the bottom 'power' line, i.e. help them to lose interest in the development.

Choose your Tony tactic

Once you have identified people/institutions to target, you need to decide on the best method to do this. Many groups do this by plunging straight into discussing the first one or two ideas that people come up with. Often they get stuck there for hours and time runs out before other (more interesting) options can be explored. This approach not only limits the choice of action, but also stifles creativity. You can avoid this by using the following exercise:

Tony Brainstorm

This tool helps to quickly gather a large number of ideas for actions you can do. The idea is to encourage creativity and free energy. Begin with stating the issue to be tackled. Ask people to say whatever comes into their heads as fast as possible—without censoring it. The crazier the ideas the better. This helps people to be inspired by each other. Have one or two note takers to write all the ideas down where everyone can see them. Make sure there is no discussion or comment on others' ideas. Structured thinking and organizing can come afterwards. After the people run out of ideas check over the list of actions that has been generated and clarify any that aren't understandable. Now you can move on to discussing the advantages and disadvantages of the different ideas. Make sure you don't discount crazier ideas out of hand. Sometimes these are the ones with the most potential. A good way of analyzing actions is the:

Developing the plan

By now you should have a good idea of what kind of actions and tactics you want to go for. The next exercise helps you to form them into a time plan.

Time Line

The purpose of a time-line is to give you an idea of how many different things you may have to do, and when. In this example a group wants to set up a resource center for local people and community groups to use. Starting off with lots of activity may be tempting but if this means that after two months everyone is burnt out, you should think again. It is definitely worth checking how much time people in the group are willing to give to the project. As time goes on you might want to intensify your activities and increase the pressure by choosing more tactics. List all the activities of your group. What was good, what didn't work so well? What could be done differently in the future? Be aware that what some people feel to be negative might be a positive thing for others. It isn't necessary to agree on this.

When people are disillusioned and frustrated, it helps to look at the successes the group has had. When there is still a mountain of work to be done, it is easy to forget what has been achieved. Just put up a large piece of paper and ask people to list any successes, however small. These could be a mention in the newspaper, a successful fundraising event, making links with other groups, publishing a pamphlet. On a personal level people may have learnt new skills, feel more confident, got to know new people.

Other things to consider

Burnout

If you use these tools properly, they can help you to avoid burnout. If you notice that anyone in your group is getting tired out, then see how they can pass on some of their responsibilities. If that isn't possible then re-evaluate your plans so that they're less intense. Everyone should be aware of their own personal limits, and not take on too much—again by mapping out your plans you can take account of people's limits and availability.

Underlying Values

When considering aims and tactics one question regularly crops up—is your group wanting to improve the existing society or does it want to achieve a fundamental change in the way society works? People also have widely varying ideas about how change happens and this will influence the tactics they choose. However most groups mix their tactics and tools, regardless of political persuasion. For many mainstream groups direct action has become more acceptable and is often used to attract the media.

How change happens

The key to effective grassroots lobbying and campaigning is communication and action Communication and action is the core of any grassroots program, and the way we communicate and act is just as important as what we say and do. There are several methods of grassroots lobbying and campaigning. However, using the right one at the appropriate time is essential to have an impact on the legislative and electoral process.

When was the last time you contacted your U.S. Senators, Representative or candidate running for a federal office to tell them how you felt about an issue? Never. Well, you are not alone! Surveys show, for example, that 90 percent of American adults have never written a letter to a Member of Congress.

Suggested Grassroots Activities during a political campaign cycle:

Ask local and state clubs to mail at least one pro-X (Candidate) piece and one piece to their memberships before Election Day. This could either be a personalized letter from the president or a campaign flyer.

Organize a phone bank to do ID/persuasion and OR work with a campaign/candidate to have their phone bank one night per week.

Get locals to issue press releases endorsing Candidate X Leaflet on bulletin boards. Place yard signs in targeted precincts, especially near polling places. Ask the candidate you are supporting or your local Coordinated Campaign for targeted precincts. Organize and conduct literature drops in targeted precincts. This involves preparing maps and materials. Ask the candidate you are supporting or your local Coordinated Campaign for targeted precincts.

Distribute information on your candidate at community events like county fairs, church bazaars, school nights, local festivals, etc.

Conduct a "Letters to the Editor" campaign on behalf of you candidate.

Issue press releases for candidate X events to local and external news outlets.

Canvass door-to-door in targeted precincts with candidate X flyers.

Speak at regular events in the community in support of Candidate X, e.g. Rotary Clubs, Kiwanis Clubs, Chamber of Commerce, etc.

Election Day:

Dispatch volunteers to be poll workers outside the polling place. Poll workers usually distribute voter slate cards and make sure signs are displayed outside the polling site.

- Organize rides to the polls.
- Organize and/or staff phone banks.
- Distribute slate cards and/or door hangers in targeted precincts before the polls open.
- Put up yard signs in precincts with polling places.

One important piece of information that I'd like to add is a report that I came across that deals with a question that is "bugging everyone",

Are there differences in voting behavior between Naturalized and Native born Americans? As you review this information keep an open mind and remember that change begins with a purpose and a goal of success. Thanks to the Census bureau for providing this report, which also reveals trends of voting patterns.

12

AFTERTHOUGHTS

Tony & Mrs. Welsh

After reviewing my book titled *Rising Tide*, hopefully some of your thoughts or questions have been answered. Sections in this book covered the basics, and it should be stated that politics on the East and West coasts can be very different.

But one thing is uniform, family and close bonds work hand and hand with everything. Political musings serve as examples and the Tony Tactics serve as core guidelines that I've followed in my last run for the State House of Texas. The recipes listed in the back have come from my families' special brew of secrets that have been passed from one generation to the next. Each generation lives in order that the children and great grandchildren will live with the most important thing—Tradition.

While sitting at the breakfast table, I read the Dallas Morning News and went straight to the Metro section and reviewed an interesting article discussing the outcome of the primary elections in Dallas County in March 2006. The interesting point made, was that each party was criticized for not preparing for the election. Republican and Democrat alike failed to overcome the style of politicking that requires grassroots and basic footwork. Basic concepts in every election, the simple tactics covered in chapters ten and eleven, the chapters explain that footwork is required. The illusion that your name and political powers protect your election is false. I've listed some examples from the March 14, 2006 article; Gromer Jeffers Jr. explained it like this.

> "In a low turnout election, an entrenched, scandal free incumbent is not supposed to lose. Even in the bland political environs of Dallas, the precinct soldier's primary job is to deliver for the party. They didn't deliver last Tuesday, and the incumbents paid the price. Mr.Grusendorf bragged that he had the support of every precinct chair in his district, except for his ex wife, Barbara Thompson-Grusendorf. He also had the backing of Tarrant County Republican Party Chairwoman Stephanie Klick, Gov.Rick Perry and House Speaker Tom Craddick. Yet, university professor Diane Patrick gave him a clear beat down. After almost 20 years in the Legislature, Mr. Grusendorf should have had a political operation that could have withstood the school finance backlash. Or maybe not, because local patronage and other tools that historically hold political groups together."

So this serves as a forecast to others out there, don't wait for the magical powers of the establishment to put you in office. Grassroots and strategy will take it, over flashy names placed on mailers and group chants of go team. Work must also come with the mission, having twenty consultants and campaign advisors, along with a team of thinkers, is going to accomplish one thing. It will show the obvious, which is, wow! This was a very expensive election. If pouring money into a project that has a return of ten percent, divided by two. What have we accomplished? Vegas pays better then the five percent payout.

I am not going to just attack the republicans on this, Gromer Jeffers Jr. stated it in the second half "The biggest collapse of political infrastructure came from southern sector democrats. Ms. Caraway had an eight year record on the council, lots of energy and a campaign photo that made her look like a starlet. But Dallas County Commissioner John Wiley Price, state Sen. Royce West, former Dallas Mayor Ron Kirk, state Rep. Yvonne Davis and others supported Mr. Jones, who served in the legislature since 1993." Gromer goes on to conclude, "State lawmakers, though, must get back to building political organizations that can deliver votes. Otherwise, their notoriety will come only after embarrassing losses."

Well its clearly stated that weak teams and structure fail every time. The Southwest is experiencing a decay of its political structure, and organization. Had they read the book before the election, they may have had a chance at victory. The Tide is rising, and it is up to each individual out there to get out and extend a hand and get involved in the basic duty of giving back to the community. City council races, school board races, even the local PTA. Enjoy my recipes and drop me a note on your thoughts. Questions that I'll leave you with are does Arnold win using his old strategy, for his second term as governor and run for the senate? Will the Southwest prepare itself for the changing demographics, and learn to change with the times?

Will the war in Iraq play a lasting effect on future politics with all the returning veterans of the war? Which by the way, will be explained in my book titled Iron Horse, the fight for Sadr City, look for it to come out in the fall. It details my experience in Baghdad, Iraq during the fight for East Baghdad.

In closing I'd like to give a big Thanks to the Medical staff at Mesquite Medical Center for doing the best job in the area.

13

CULTURE AND FOOD

"There are people in the world so hungry,
that God cannot appear to them except in the form of bread."
—Mahatma Gandhi 1869–1948

Music and dance of Latin America "crossed over" into American culture. Mexican mariachi bands—small ensembles usually consisting of violins, guitars, and trumpets—have long enjoyed popularity in the United States. Dances and dance music from the Caribbean islands, especially Cuba, were first performed in American ballrooms in the late 1900's. Some popular Cuban dances have included the bomba, the cha-cha, the conga, the mambo, the rumba, and salsa. Much of the music and dancing was derived from the culture of African slaves who worked on West Indian sugar plantations from the early 1500's to the 1800's. The music has instruments of African and American Indian origin, including conga drums, claves, guiros, maracas, and marimbas.

Music has always been the ambassador to merging communities. Latin-American music has long been an important influence on the popular music of the United States. Since the 1940's, a number of Hispanic-American rock music performers have gained widespread popularity, including Ritchie Valens, Carlos Santana, Gloria Estefan, and the group Los Lobos. Traditional Latin music has also attracted a large audience in the United States. One of the most popular performers of traditional Latin music was Celia Cruz. Known as la Reina de la Salsa (the Queen of Salsa), Cruz has performed for more than 40 years in both Cuba and the United States. She will always be remembered for the good that she performed.

A number of painters and writers have sought to capture the Hispanic American experience. Important Hispanic artists include John Valadez, Martin Ramirez, Frank Romero, and Arnaldo Roche. Tomas Rivera, Luis Valdez, and Heberto Padilla rank among the many Hispanic writers who have won distinction. Other major Hispanic American figures in the arts include architect Alberto Vargas of Monterrey, Mexico. I had the opportunity to visit with this artist in his private Vila in the mountains. Our discussions revealed grand visions about the future and certain influences with his work that dealt with the struggle of society, he currently travels to Europe and studies the architecture of the famous Churches.

Since the 1970's, however, TV shows, movies, and plays that deal more realistically with Hispanic characters have appealed to both Hispanic and non-Hispanic audiences. Hispanic actors are now able to play roles that previously would have been reserved for English-speaking actors. Successful Hispanic actors and actresses have included Melissa Quirk who has worked in Dallas for some time and Corrine Cruz who sings Jazz in some of the area clubs north of Austin. Anthony Quinn, Antonio Aguilar. Hispanics share the American enthusiasm for sports, soccer, football, golf, baseball, stockcar and Formula One racing. A number of Hispanic athletes have become professional sports stars. Well-known Hispanic athletes include baseball greats Rafael Palmero, Roberto Clemente, Jose Canseco, and Fernando Valenzuela; golfers Nancy Lopez and Lee Trevino.

Hispanics observe major holidays of their homelands in addition to U.S. holidays. Mexican Americans celebrate the anniversary of Mexico's independence from Spain on September 16. Which is really the greatest day in Mexico and throughout the southwest, and growing everyday in the area compared to the Cinco de Mayo festival, which commemorates Mexico's victory in a small fight with the Foreign Legion in some desolate frontier post. How this ever became the flagship of holidays is a surprise to me. Cuban Americans celebrate Cuban Independence Day on May 20; the date Cuba gained its independence from Spain in 1898. As for a record, most Cubans also celebrate the day of future freedom without a Fidel Castro.

The United States observes National Hispanic Heritage Month each year from September 15 to October 15, when many Latin-American countries celebrate their independence. Besides Mexico, these countries include Costa Rica, El Salvador, Guatemala, Honduras, and Nicaragua. Some cities with large Hispanic communities hold annual festivals featuring the arts and crafts, food, and music and dancing of Latin America. These festivals include Miami's nine-day Calle Ocho, held in March of each year, and the Fiesta de la Primavera, held in San Diego in May. Other Hispanic festivals are held at Christmas and Easter and on other religious holidays. One of the largest of these festivals is the nine-day Mexican Christmas festival of Las posadas, which features songs and processions commemorating Mary and Joseph's search for an inn in Bethlehem.

I can remember a time when my sisters where in a church program and the priest walked over to Kathy and said "my dear, would you give your seat to the baby Jesus and she said yes, just as long a she could sit down on the same chair as Anna. Kathy's favorite holiday activity would be getting up early in the morning and making Mexican Bread with my mother. It is a long tradition to be the first, to bake in the New Year. Somehow, it is suppose to bring good luck. Good Luck, is being able to share with others and remembering the similarities that unite us. So, my mother states.

Father Eades & Father Sullivan

Remember that food preparation is very religious,
each process must be followed to ensure total salvation.
Mama Aguilar

Tio Franco Chile

Green Chile should have the tough, transparent outer skin removed before it is used. The process is simple and may be done as follows:

Fresh Green Chile

Rinse and dry Chile. Prick Chile with the tines of a fork to allow for release of steam.

Place Chile on a cookie sheet 4-6 inches below the broiling element.

Turn Chile frequently until it is uniformly blistered.

Remove Chile from the broiler and cover with a damp towel for 10 minutes.

Proceed with one of the steps below:

- When cooled, package chilies in a freezer-weight container, seal, and freeze for later use.

- Remove the outer skin and freeze as in step A.

- Remove outer skin, stem, and seeds. Chop and use in any recipe.

- Remove outer skin and leave Chile whole for freezing, drying, or use in a recipe.

Don Chile Verde

- 1 tablespoon shortening 1 cup chicken broth**

- 1/2 cup chopped onion 1/4 teaspoon garlic powder

- 2 tablespoons flour 3/4 teaspoon salt

- 1 cup chopped green Chile*

1. Heat shortening in a medium-sized skillet on medium heat. Sauté the chopped onion in shortening. Add flour and cook for 1 minute. Add all remaining ingredients and simmer for 20 minutes.* Varied amounts may be used.

2. ** Two cups tomatoes with liquid may be substituted.

Don Salsa Verde

- 1 large tomato, chopped Chopped green Chile*

- 1 small onion, chopped

- 1/2 teaspoon garlic salt

1. Combine all ingredients in a medium-sized mixing bowl and marinate for at least 15 minutes.

2. *Varied amounts may be used.

Chile Verde Seco

- 10-12 dried green chilies, 1 cup canned tomatoes

- Hot water (optional), 1 pound pork steak, cubed

- 1/4 teaspoon garlic powder, 2-3 cups water

- 1/2 teaspoon salt,

1. Place Chile in a large mixing bowl and cover Chile with water. Set aside for 5-10 minutes. Remove stems and seeds from Chile. Chop Chile finely and set aside.

2. Brown pork in a medium-sized skillet on medium heat. Drain and add Chile, 2-3 cups of water, tomatoes, and seasonings. Simmer at low heat for 10-15 minutes.

All red Chile recipes are prepared from native grown Chile. Canned, red Chile powder available in the "spice section" of grocery stores should not be substituted. {Usually prepared chili, chili powders, and salsas contain a lot of ingredients that are not Chile. AND, different Chile peppers have different tastes.)Rinse and dry Chile pods. Remove seeds, if desired. Place Chile pods on a cookie sheet in a 250°F oven for approximately 10 minutes.Turn Chile pods several times to avoid scorching (the Chile pods will turn a deeper red).The toasted Chile pods may be used for preparing red Chile powder, or Chile sauce (see below).

Maria Chavell Molido

- 16 dried red Chile pods, stems removed

1. Place 2-3 pods in a blender container and finely grind them on low speed.

2. Add more pods until the lower portion of the jar is full.

3. Empty container and continue to process until all pods are ground.

Tito Martin Caribe

- 1-2 cups water, 8-10 toasted red Chile pods*

1. Place water and Chile pods in large saucepan.

2. Heat to boiling on high heat.

3. Pour mixture into a blender container and process to a smooth consistency.

4. * Preparation of Dried Red Chile Pods recipe above.

   NOTE: Chile Caribe may be used as a base for any Chile recipe.

Tia Anita Colorado

- 2 tablespoons shortening 3/4 teaspoon salt 2 tablespoons flour 1/2 teaspoon garlic salt ¼–3/4 cup Red Chile Powder*Oregano (optional) 2 cups cold water** Comino (optional) Heat shortening in a medium saucepan on medium heat. Stir in flour and cook for 1 minute. Add Chile powder and cook for an additional minute.Gradually add the water and stir, making sure that no lumps form. Add seasonings to sauce and simmer at low heat for 10-15 minutes.* Red Chile recipe above. Varied amounts and variety of Chile will determine the degree of hotness. One to two cups Chile Caribe may be substituted. ** For a milder flavor, tomato juice may be substituted.

1. NOTE: One pound of cooked beef or pork, ground, cubed, or shredded, may be added.

San Rosa Guacamole

- 2 large, ripe avocados, peeled and pitted
- Chopped green Chile* 1 1/2 teaspoons lime juice
- 1 tomato, minced 1/4 teaspoon garlic powder
- 1-2 green onions, minced 1/2 teaspoon salt

1. Mash avocados and mix with remaining ingredients.

2. Serve with tostados.** * Varied amounts may be used.

San Angelo Tostados

- Shortening, Garlic Salt 12 Corn Tortillas*
- Red Chile Powder* (optional) Salt (optional)

1. Heat 2-inches of shortening in a heavy pan at medium-high heat. Cut tortillas into quarters to within 1/2 inch from center of tortilla.

2. Fry tortillas until crisp and drain well on absorbent towels. Separate each tortilla into four tostados.

3. Tostados may be sprinkled with salt, garlic salt, or Chile powder.

San Luis Potosi Nachos

- 48 Tostados* 1/2 cup sour cream 6 ounces jalapeno cheese** 48 pieces jalapeno Chile cut into 1-inch squares Red Chile Powder*(optional.)

1. Place tostados on baking sheets. Top each tostado with a square of cheese. Spoon 1/2 teaspoon of sour cream on top of each piece of cheese.

2. Top with a piece of Chile and sprinkle with Chile powder. Heat in a 450&degree;F oven for 2-3 minutes, or until the cheese melts. Serve warm.

3. ** Monterey Jack cheese may be substituted.

Rosie San Miguel con Queso

- 1 cup grated American cheese 1 medium tomato, chopped 1/2 cup grated sharp cheddar cheese
- Chopped green Chile*1/8 teaspoon garlic powder
- 1/4 cup cream, approximately in medium-weight pan melt cheese on low heat. Add cream and stir constantly to prevent scorching.Stir in tomato, Chile, and garlic powder. Add more cream if needed to reach dipping consistency.Serve warm with tostados**

1. * Varied amounts may be used.

Ludivina Reyna Rellenos Dulces

- Shortening, 1 cup chopped raisins,

- 1 egg

- 1 1/2 teaspoons allspice,

- 2 pounds beef or pork, boiled and ground 1 teaspoon salt

- 1 cup chopped green Chile*

- 1 1/2 cups brown sugar

- 1 cup flour Heat 2-inches of shortening in a heavy pan on medium-high heat.

- Beat egg and milk in a small mixing bowl. Set aside.Combine meat, sugar, raisins, allspice, salt, and Chile with 2 tablespoons of egg mixture.

- Form mixture into 1/2-inch balls. Dip balls into remaining egg mixture and roll in flour.Fry sweet Chile meatballs in hot shortening until golden.

- Drain on absorbent towels.

Yamily Empanaditas de Chorizo

- Pastry for 9-inch, double crust pie,

- 3 tablespoons sour cream

- 5-6 ounces chorizo (Mexican Sausage)

- 2 tablespoons chopped green Chile*

1. Roll pastry to a 1/8-inch thickness on a lightly floured board.

2. Cut pastry into circles that is 3 inches in diameter. Set aside. Remove casings from chorizo.

3. Fry chorizo in a small skillet at medium heat. Drain. Combine chorizo, sour cream, and Chile in a small mixing bowl.

4. Place a spoonful of mixture, off center, on each pastry circle.

5. Fold pastry in half over filling, and pinch edges together to seal.Pierce top of turnovers with tines of a fork.

6. Place empanaditas on an ungreased baking sheet and bake in a 450-degree oven for 10-12 minutes or until golden.

7. * Varied amounts may be used.

John Z. Gonzales Jicama

- 1 tablespoon salt
- 1-2 pounds jicama, peeled and thinly sliced
- 1/4 teaspoon Red Chile Powder*
- 1 lime, cut in wedges

1. Combine salt and Chile powder in a small serving bowl
2. Arrange jicama on a serving tray with the bowl of seasonings and lime wedges.
3. To eat, rub lime over jicama and dip it into seasoning.
4. *Varied amounts may be used.

Zacatecas Pintos

- 2 cups dried pinto beans
- 1/2 teaspoon garlic salt
- 9 cups water 2 tablespoons lard or shortening
- 1 teaspoon salt,
- Sort pinto beans and rinse in cold water. Place beans and water in a large stewing pot.
- Bring mixture to a boil over high heat. Reduce heat to medium and cook until beans are tender.

1. Add seasonings and shortening to beans and simmer at low heat for an additional 30 minutes.
2. *Variations:* Salt pork, tomatoes, tomato sauce, catsup, or onions may be added for additional flavor.
3. ** Frijoles Pintos may be cooked in a pressure cooker for 45 minutes at 15 pounds pressure, seasoned, and simmered at low heat for an additional 30 minutes.

Frasica Frijoles

- 1/2 cup shortening ½–1 cup bean liquid
- 4 cups cooked pinto beans 2 cups grated sharp cheddar cheese Heat shortening in a medium-sized skillet at medium heat.

1. Add beans and liquid to the shortening.
2. Mash beans and cook for 10-15 minutes.
3. Add 1 1/2 cups cheese to the beans and stir for 2-3 minutes at low heat.
4. Garnish with remaining cheese before serving.

Mi Papas Con Chile

- 2 cups potatoes, peeled and thinly sliced, 1/2 teaspoon Red Chile Powder* 2 tablespoons shortening 1 clove garlic, minced 2 tablespoons flour
- 1/2 teaspoon salt 3 1/2 cups water Brown potatoes in shortening in a medium-sized skillet at medium heat. Remove potatoes from skillet. Add flour and brown slightly. Mix Chile, garlic, and salt with flour and add potatoes and water.Simmer for 10-15 minutes at low heat.

1. *Varied amounts may be used.

Dos Papas Con Chile

- 2 cups potatoes, peeled and thinly sliced
- 1/2 teaspoon garlic salt
- 1/2 teaspoon salt
- 2 tablespoons shortening
- 1/2 cup chopped green Chile*
- 1/4 cup chopped onions
- 2 cups water

1. Brown potatoes in shortening in a medium-sized skillet at medium heat.
2. Add onions and seasonings and cook until onions are tender.
3. Add green Chile and water and simmer for 15-20 minutes at low heat. *

4.   Varied amounts may be used.

Mi Mal Español

- 1/4 cup chopped onion 1/8 teaspoon oregano
- 2 tablespoons shortening 1/4 teaspoon garlic salt
- 6 ounces Spanish-style tomato sauce
- 2 teaspoons shortening 1 cup raw rice, rinsed until water is clear 1 cup chicken broth 1 1/2 teaspoons salt
- 3 cups chicken broth Place onion and 2 tablespoons of shortening in a medium-sized saucepan.

1.   Sauté onion at medium heat until transparent.

2.   Add tomato sauce, 1-cup chicken broth, salt, oregano, and garlic salt to onion and simmer mixture at low heat for 1 hour. Set aside.

3.   Add 3 cups chicken broth to rice and bring to a boil using medium-high heat.

4.   Reduce heat to low, cover and simmer for 20 minutes, or until the broth is absorbed.

5.   Place shortening and rice in a large skillet.

6.   Stir-fry rice at low heat until the rice is browned, approximately 15 minutes.

7.   Combine sauce and rice and serve warm.

Gazpacho Loco

- 1 Cup tomato juice 4 lg tomatoes, peeled and finely chopped 2 T wine vinegar
- 3 T Olive oil 1 lg cucumber, finely chopped
- 1/4 t garlic salt
- 1/2 t salt 2-3 T finely chopped green Chile*
- 1 med onion, finely chopped

- Black pepper to taste Combine all ingredients in a medium-sized mixing bowl. Chill at least 1 hour before serving. To serve, pour into small lettuce-lined bowls.

Tejas Tortillas

- 4 cups flour
- 4 tablespoons shortening
- 2 teaspoons salt
- 1 1/2 cups warm water, approximately
- 2 teaspoons baking powder

1. Combine dry ingredients in a medium-sized mixing bowl and cut in shortening.

2. Make a well in center of dry ingredients. Add water, a small amount at a time, and work mixture into a dough.

3. Knead dough until smooth, cover, and set aside for 10 minutes.

4. Form dough into balls the size of an egg. Roll each ball of dough into a circle 6 inches in diameter.

5. Heat a griddle or skillet on medium-high heat. Place each tortilla on griddle and cook for approximately 1 minute on each side. (Tortilla should be lightly speckled.)

Tortillas De Maiz

- 2 cups blue or yellow corn Masa Harina*
- 1 teaspoon salt 1 2/3 cups boiling water

1. Combine Masa Harina and salt in a medium-sized mixing bowl. Add boiling water and stir until dough resembles, thick, cooked cereal.Wet hands and form dough into balls the size of an egg.Place each ball of dough between two lightly moistened pieces of waxed paper and flatten to about 1/8 inch thick, using a tortilla press, rolling pin, or pressure from the hands Remove tortilla from waxed paper. Heat griddle or skillet on medium-high heat. Place each tortilla on the griddle and cook for approximately 1 minute on each side. (Tortillas should be lightly speck-

led.)* Masa Harina is available in the cereal section of most grocery stores.

Pan De Maiz Con Jalapeno

- 1 cup flour
- 2 eggs 1/4 cup sugar
- 1 cup milk 1 tablespoon baking powder
- 1/4 cup shortening 1 teaspoon salt
- 8 ounces cream-style corn 1/4 teaspoon garlic powder
- 2 tablespoons chopped jalapeno Chile*/**
- 1 cup yellow cornmeal Combine first six ingredients in a medium-sized mixing bowl. Add eggs, milk, and shortening to flour mixture and beat until smooth.

1. Add corn and pepper and blend well.
2. Pour mixture into a greased, 8-inch baking pan
3. Bake in a 425°F oven for 35-40 minutes, or until cornbread is golden brown.
4. * Varied amounts may be used.
5. **Two tablespoons of chopped green Chile may be substituted.

Enchiladas de Queso

- 12 corn tortillas* 2 onions chopped Shortening
- 2 cups coarsely chopped lettuce (optional)
- 4 cups Red or Green Chile sauce* 3 cups grated sharp cheddar cheese

1. Heat 1/2 inch of shortening in a heavy pan at medium-high heat.
2. Quickly dip each tortilla into the shortening to soften.
3. Drain on absorbent towels.
4. Assemble the enchiladas by placing 1/4-cup sauce on each dinner place, followed by a tortilla (tortilla can be rolled after filling is placed on it), 1/4-cup sauce, 1/4-cup cheese, and onion. Repeat twice. Top with

remaining sauce. 4. Place in 350°F oven for 15 minutes, or until the cheese melts. Garnish with lettuce. NOTE: Traditionally, enchiladas are topped with a fried or poached egg before serving.

Chimichangas de Pollo

- 1 3 1/2 pound whole chicken 1/4 teaspoon crushed leaf oregano, 6 cups water 1 medium onion, studded with 2 whole cloves, 1/4 teaspoon crushed leaf basil 1/8 teaspoon cinnamon 2 stalks celery 8 Four Tortillas, warmed** 2 large whole garlic cloves, peeled Shortening 2 cups sour cream (optional) 1 bay leaf 1 cup Guacamole***(optional)

- 2 tablespoons shortening 2 cups grated cheddar cheese, 1 large onion, thinly sliced (optional) 1 garlic clove, minced, Shredded lettuce (optional) tomato wedges (optional) 1 large tomato, cored and diced 1 jalapeno Chile* 1 teaspoon salt 1/8 teaspoon black pepper, Place the chicken, water, onion, celery, 2 garlic cloves, and bay leaf in a medium-sized stewing pot. Cook chicken at medium heat for approximately 1 1/2 hours, or until the chicken is tender.

1. Allow chicken to cool, remove meat from bones, and chop. (Broth from chicken may be reserved for future use).

2. Place shortening, sliced onion, and 1 minced garlic clove in a medium-sized skillet and sauté mixture at medium heat until onion is tender.Add the chopped chicken, tomato, jalapeno Chile, and remaining seasonings and simmer at low heat for 10-15 minutes. Place approximately 1/2 cup of chicken mixture horizontally across the bottom half of each tortilla.

3. Do not extend the mixture beyond 1 1/2 inches at the sides and bottom. Fold the sides in over the filling and roll the tortilla jellyroll style. Secure each roll with a toothpick.

4. Heat 2-inches of shortening in a heavy pan at medium-high heat. Fry each rolled tortilla in hot shortening until crisp and lightly browned. Drain on absorbent towels.

5. Assemble the chimichangas by placing each rolled tortilla on a plate and garnish with 1/4 cup of sour cream, 2 tablespoons of guacamole, 1/3 cup of cheddar cheese, lettuce, and tomato wedges.* Varied amounts may be used. Chopped green Chile may be substituted.

6. ** Thin, commercial flour tortillas are easier to roll. Tortillas must be warmed in order to roll them without tearing.

7. *** See recipe for Flour Tortillas and Guacamole.

Chiles Rellenos

- Shortening
- Batter for Stuffed Green Chile (see below)
- 12 large, peeled, whole green chilies with stems
- Red or Green Chile Sauce*
- 1 pound sharp cheddar cheese, cut into strips

Heat 4 inches of shortening in a heavy pan on medium-high heat.
Slit chilies open crosswise below stems.
Insert strips of cheese into chilies.
Dip stuffed Chile into batter and fry in hot shortening until golden brown. Drain on absorbent towels.
Serve with red or green Chile sauce.

Batido para Chile Rellenos

- 1 cup flour, 3/4 cup cornmeal, 1 teaspoon baking powder, 1 cup milk, approximately, more may be added for smooth batter, 1/2 teaspoon salt
- 2 eggs, slightly beaten, Combine flour, baking powder, salt, and cornmeal in a medium-sized bowl.

1. Blend milk with eggs and add to dry ingredients. Mix well. Proceed with step 4 above (Chiles Rellenos recipe.)

Tamales

- Corn Husks,Masa*,Water,Chile con Carne para Tamales * * Recipes below.

Assembling Tamales

1. Rinse cornhusks and soak in warm water until pliable.

2. Spread the center portion of each husk with 2 tablespoons of masa mixture.

3. Top with 1 tablespoon* of meat-meat filling.

4. Fold the sides of the husk toward the center, the bottom of the husk up, and the top down. Tie each tamale with a cornhusk strip. Pour 2 inches of water into a large steamer. Arrange tamales on a rack in steamer above the water level.

5. Steam tamales for 45 minutes (Longer at high altitudes. May also be steamed in a pressure cooker for 20 minutes at 15 pounds pressure.)

6. * Varied amounts may be used.

*Masa

- 6 cups masa harina*
- 2 cups lard
- 3 1/2 cups warm water, approximately
- 2 teaspoons salt

1. Combine the Masa Harina and water in a large mixing bowl to make masa. Set aside.

2. Cream the lard and salt in a medium-sized mixing bowl using a mixer at medium speed.

3. Add the creamed lard to the masa and mix well.

4. * Six cups commercially prepared masa may be substituted and the water omitted. Masa Harina is available in the cereal section of most grocery stores.

Chile Con Carne Para Tamales

- 1 1/2 pounds beef or pork, stewed and shredded
- 2 cups meat broth 1/2 teaspoon salt
- 2 tablespoons lard 1/8 teaspoon oregano
- 1 tablespoon flour 1/4 teaspoon comino

- 1/2 cup Red Chile Powder*1/2 teaspoon garlic salt

1. Combine meat and lard in a large skillet and fry meat at medium heat until browned.

2. Add the flour to meat and cook for 1 minute, stirring constantly. Add the Chile powder, broth, and seasonings to the meat. Cook at medium heat for approximately 30 minutes, stirring constantly until the mixture has thickened.

3. * See Red Chile Powder recipe. *Varied amounts may be used.

Carne Adovada

- 4 cloves garlic
- 2 recipes Chile Caribe*
- 1 tablespoon salt
- 5 pounds lean pork steaks
- 1 tablespoon oregano

1. Add garlic, salt, and oregano to Chile caribe.

2. Place pork steaks in large, glass baking dish and pour Chile caribe mixture over steaks.

3. Cover and refrigerate for 8-24 hours.

4. Place drained, marinated steaks in a 350°F oven and roast for 40-60 minutes.

5. Serve with heated remaining Chile caribe.

6. *See recipe for Chile Caribe.

Pozole

- 1 pound prepared pozole corn, thoroughly rinsed**
- 1 medium onion, chopped 2 cloves garlic, minced
- 10 cups water, 1/4 teaspoon oregano

- 1 pound pork or beef roast*** 1 teaspoon ground comino, 5 cups water, approximately 3-6 dried red Chile pods, rinsed and crumbled**** 2 tablespoons salt

1. Place pozole and 10 cups water in large stewing pot. Bring mixture to a boil at high heat.

2. Reduce heat to low and simmer pozole for 5 hours.

3. Approximately 1 hour before the completion of the simmering time, brown the pork in a large, heavy skillet on medium heat.

4. Add the pork to the stewing pot with 5 cups of water and continue to cook on low heat until tender.

5. Add the remaining ingredients to pozole and simmer for an additional 1-2 hours. Adjust seasonings to suit taste. * Pozole may be cooked in a pressure cooker for 45 minutes at 15 pounds pressure. ** Pozole corn is marketed dry or prepared. ** Varied amounts may be used. **** If desired, omit Chile pods and serve with Red Chile Sauce or Green Chile Sauce.

Guisado de Chile Verde

- 2 pounds pork or beef, cubed, 3 cups tomatoes
- 1/4 cup flour, 2 cups water, 2 tablespoons shortening
- 1/2 teaspoon garlic powder, 2 large onions, chopped
- 2 teaspoons salt, 3 cups chopped green Chile*

1. Dredge the meat in flour.

2. Place the shortening in a heavy skillet and brown meat at medium heat.

3. Place meat in a large stewing pot.

4. Sauté the onions in the remaining shortening and add to stewing pot.

5. Add all remaining ingredients to stewing pot and simmer at low heat for 1 hour.

6. * Varied amounts may be used.

Menudo

- 2 pounds tripe 2 tablespoons chopped onions
- Water, 2 tablespoons flour 2 tablespoons shortening
- 1/8 teaspoon garlic salt 2 eggs, separated

1. Place tripe in a large saucepan and cover it with water. Simmer at low heat until tripe is tender.

2. Drain tripe and reserve liquid.

3. Remove and discard fatty portions of tripe and cut tripe into 1-inch pieces. Set aside. Sauté onion in shortening in a medium-sized saucepan at medium heat. Set aside.

4. Beat egg whites until stiff in a small mixing bowl.

5. Add egg yolks and continue to beat until mixture is lemon colored. Add flour and salt and mix well.

6. Fold cooked tripe into egg mixture.

7. Add tripe mixture to saucepan containing sautéed onions. Cook at medium heat until eggs are set.

8. Add reserved liquid from tripe and garlic salt to egg mixture and simmer at low heat for 5-10 minutes.

Postres Arroz Dulce

- 1 cup rice 1 cup raisins
- 2 cups water 3 eggs separated
- 1 teaspoon salt 3/4 teaspoons vanilla
- 2 cups evaporated milk 1/4 teaspoon cinnamon
- 3/4 cups sugar 1/4 teaspoon nutmeg (optional)

1. Combine the rice, water, and salt in a large saucepan.

2. Bring the water to a boil at high heat. Cover saucepan.

3. Reduce heat to low and continue to cook for 12-15 minutes, or until the water is absorbed. Combine milk, sugar and egg yolks and add to

rice. Add raisins, vanilla, and cinnamon, and simmer for 5 minutes. Remove from heat.

4. Beat the egg whites until stiff and fold into the rice.

5. Chill and garnish with nutmeg before serving.

Flan Caramelisado

- 2 cups sugar 6 eggs 3 1/2 cups milk
- 1 teaspoon vanilla 1 cinnamon stick

1. Place 1 cup of sugar in a heavy pan. Stir sugar at low heat until it is liquid and light, golden brown.

2. Pour caramelized sugar evenly into six warm custard cups. Set cups aside. Place milk and cinnamon stick in a medium-sized saucepan. Scald milk at medium heat and allow cooling.

3. Beat eggs until foamy. Gradually add remaining sugar to eggs and beat well.Gradually add scalded milk to egg mixture, stirring until sugar dissolves. Add vanilla.

4. Pour mixture into caramel-lined cups.

5. Place cups in a pan of hot water and bake in a 350°F oven for 1 hour and 10 minutes.

Natillas

- 4 eggs, separated
- 1/8 teaspoon salt
- 1/4 cup flour
- Nutmeg
- 4 cups milk
- Cinnamon
- 3/4 cup sugar

1. Place egg yolks, flour, and 1 cup of milk in a small mixing bowl. Stir to make a smooth paste. Set aside.

2. Place the remaining milk, sugar, and salt in a medium-sized saucepan and scald at medium heat.

3. Add the egg mixture to the scalded milk and continue to cook at medium heat until a soft custard consistency is reached.

4. Remove custard from heat and allow to cool to room temperature.

5. Beat the egg whites in a medium-sized mixing bowl until they are stiff, but not dry.

6. Fold the egg whites into the custard, chill, and garnish with nutmeg and cinnamon before serving.

Mrs. Priolo, & Sister Veronica

BIBLIOGRAPHY

Alba, Richard and Victor Nee. 1997. "Rethinking Assimilation Theory for a New Era of Immigration." International Migration Review. Vol. 31:4. (Winter).

Callis, Robert. 1997. "Immigration Bolsters U.S. Housing Market." Census Brief. CENBR/97-4. Washington, DC: U.S. Government Printing Office.

Casper, Lynne M. and Loretta E. Bass. 1998. "Voting and Registration in the Election of November 1996." Current Population Reports P-20-504. Washington, DC: U.S. Bureau of the Census.

Hansen, Kristin A. 1997. "Geographical Mobility: March 1995 to March 1996." Current Population Reports P20-497. Washington, DC: U.S. Bureau of the Census.

Hansen, Kristin A. and Carol S. Faber. 1997. "The Foreign-Born Population: 1996." Current Population Reports P-20-494. Washington, DC: U.S. Government Printing Office.

Inglehart, Ronald. 1997. Modernization and Post modernization Cultural, Economic, and Political Change in 43 Societies. New Jersey: Princeton University Press.

Jennings, Jerry T. 1993. "Voting and Registration in the Election of November 1992. Current Population Reports P-20-466. Washington, DC: U.S. Gov.Printing Office. 1989. "Voting and Registration in the Election of November 1988." Current Population Reports P-20-440. Washington, DC: U.S. Government Printing Office. 1985. "Voting and Registration in the Election of November 1984." Current Population Reports P-20-405. Washington, DC: U.S. Government Printing Office. 1983. "Voting and Registration in the Election of November 1982." Current Population Reports P-20-383. Washington, DC: U.S. Government Printing Office.

Jones-Correa, Michael. 1998. "Different Paths: Gender, Immigration and Political Participation." International Migration Review. Vol. 32: 2. (Summer).

Kelley, Stanley Jr., Richard E. Ayres, and William G. Bowen. 1967. "Registration and Voting: Putting First Things First." American Political Science Review. 61: 359-79.

Kim, Jae-On, John R. Petrockik, and Stephen N. Enokson. 1975. "Voter Turnout Among the American States: Systemic and Individual Components." American Political Science Review. 69: 107-31.

Leighley, Jan E. and Jonathan Nagler. 1992. "Individual and Systemic Influences on Turnout: Who Votes?" Journal of Politics. 54: 718-40.

Lewis, Pierce, Casey McCracken, and Roger Hunt. 1994. "Politics: Who Cares?" American Demographics. Vol. 16, No. 10.

Smith, James P. and Barry Edmonston. 1997. National Academy Press. The New Americans: Economic, Demographic and Fiscal Effects of Immigration.

Squire, Peverill, Raymond E. Wolfinger, and David Glass. 1987. "Residential Mobility and Voter Turnout."American Political Science Review Vol 81:1. (March).

Teixeira, Ruy. 1992. The Disappearing American Voter. Washington, DC: The Brookings Institution.

U.S. Bureau of the Census. 1990. Census of the Population Social and Economic Characteristics. CP-2-1. Washington, DC: U.S. Government Printing Office.

Verba, Sidney and Norman H. Nie. 1972. Participation in America. New York: Harper and Row.

Wolfinger, Raymond. 1994. "Improving Voter Participation." in What to Do: Recommendations for Improving the Electoral Process. by Paul E. Frank and William G. Mayer. Boston: Northeastern University Press.

Wolfinger, Raymond and Steven J. Rosenstone. 1980. Who Votes? New Haven and London: Yale University Press.

Source: U.S. Census Bureau, Population Division, Fertility & Family Statistics Branch Authors: Loretta E. Bass and Lynne M. Casper

Rodolfo Acuña, Occupied America: A History of Chicanos (2d ed., New York: Harper and Row, 1981). Evan Anders, Boss Rule in South Texas: The Progressive Era (Austin: University of Texas Press, 1982)

Carlos E. Castañeda, Our Catholic Heritage in Texas (7 vols., Austin: Von Boeckmann-Jones, 1936-58; rpt., New York: Arno, 1976)

Gilbert R. Cruz, Let There be towns (College Station: Texas A&M University Press, 1988). Arnoldo De León, Ethnicity in the Sunbelt: A History of Mexican-Americans in Houston (University of Houston Mexican American Studies Program, 1989).

Arnoldo De León, San Angeleños: Mexican Americans in San Angelo, Texas (San Angelo: Fort Concho Museum Press, 1985)

Arnoldo De León, They Called Them Greasers: Anglo Attitudes Toward Mexicans in Texas, 1821-1900 (Austin: University of Texas Press, 1983).

Arnoldo De León and Kenneth L. Stewart, "Tejano Demographic Patterns and Socio-economic Development," Borderlands Journal 7 (Fall 1983).

Ignacio M. Garcia, United We Win: The Rise and Fall of La Raza Unida Party (Tucson: University of Arizona Mexican American Studies Research Center, 1989). Mario T. García, Desert Immigrants: The Mexicans of El Paso, 1880-1920 (New Haven: Yale University Press, 1981).

Mario T. Garcia, Mexican Americans: Leadership, Ideology, and Identity, 1930-1960 (New Haven: Yale University Press, 1989).

Richard A. García, Rise of the Mexican American Middle Class, San Antonio, 1919-1941 (College Station: Texas A&M University Press, 1991)

Gilberto Miguel Hinojosa, A Borderlands Town in Transition: Laredo, 1755-1870 (College Station: Texas A&M University Press, 1983).

Jack Jackson, Los Mesteños: Spanish Ranching in Texas, 1721-1821 (College Station: Texas A&M University Press, 1986).

Oakah L. Jones, Los Paisanos: Spanish Settlers on the Northern Frontier of New Spain (Norman: University of Oklahoma Press, 1979)

David Montejano, Anglos and Mexicans in the Making of Texas, 1836-1986 (Austin: University of Texas Press, 1987)

Manuel Peña, The Texas-Mexican Conjunto: History of a Working-Class Music (Austin: University of Texas Press, 1985)

Gerald E. Poyo and Gilberto M. Hinojosa, eds Tejano Origins in Eighteenth-Century San Antonio (San Antonio: Institute of Texan Cultures, 1991)

Guadalupe San Miguel, Jr., "Let All of Them Take Heed": Mexican Americans and the Campaign for Educational Equality in Texas (Austin: University of Texas Press, 1987). Edgar G. Shelton, Jr., Political Conditions among Texas Mexicans along the Rio Grande (M.A. thesis, University of Texas, 1946; San Francisco R&E Research Associates, 1974)

Jerry D. Thompson, Warm Weather and Bad Whiskey: The 1886 Laredo Election Riot (El Paso: Texas Western Press, 1991)

W. H. Timmons, "The El Paso Area in the Mexican Period, 1821-1848, "Southwestern Historical Quarterly 84 (July 1980).

Emilio Zamora, Mexican Labor Activity in South Texas, 1900-1920 (Ph.D. dissertation, University of Texas at Austin, 1983)

The Dallas Morning News Tuesday, March 14, 2006 Page 5B METRO "Breakdowns beat incumbents". Gromer Jeffers Jr.

Luis De-La Garza, John Zapata Gonzales, William McBurnett, Dr. Francis Hendrickson

Glory Days

Anna's Graduation SMU

Tony & Chip Moody

Kim & Katherine

Kathleen Leos & Tony

Tony, Jeb, Phil & Friends

Tony & Sheriff Boles

Dallas City Council 2003

John, Anderson, Jerry, Pham, & Tony

Tony, Cong. Sam Johnson, & Larry Sr.

Tony, Katherine & Cong. Rick Lazio (NY)

Republican State Convention Dallas

Tony, Anna & Greg

Cinco Hermanos

Gov. Rick Perry & Tony

Old' Brown Eyes

Rat Pack

Pancho & Cesar Chavez

Pancho Madranno, E. Chavez. & Anna

Dr. & Mrs. Frank Hendrickson

Mama Aguilar